Taste of Salt

Aye, Lads...

Aye, lads, so strong and bold,
    We roamed the seas like Liefs of old.
On windswept decks we groped our way
    Lashed and stung by salt and spray.
Dreams on hold, we fought, we bled,
    The cup of war we drank instead.
Those noble deeds now fiddle and flake,
    Bobbin' and tossin' in wallowing wake.
So raise once more the cup in toast,
    Salute those sons who gave their most...
'Tween slackened tongue and crusted lip
    The Taste of Salt we slowly sip.

by Theodore Treadwell

Also by Theodore R. Treadwell:

*Splinter Fleet—The Wooden Subchasers
of World War II*

Taste of Salt

❖

A WWII Skipper Looks Back

Theodore R. Treadwell
Author: Splinter Fleet—
The Wooden Subchasers
of WWII

iUniverse, Inc.
New York Lincoln Shanghai

Taste of Salt
A WWII Skipper Looks Back

Copyright © 2008 by Theodore R. Treadwell

All rights reserved. No part of this book may be used or reproduced by any means, graphic, electronic, or mechanical, including photocopying, recording, taping or by any information storage retrieval system without the written permission of the publisher except in the case of brief quotations embodied in critical articles and reviews.

iUniverse books may be ordered through booksellers or by contacting:

iUniverse
2021 Pine Lake Road, Suite 100
Lincoln, NE 68512
www.iuniverse.com
1-800-Authors (1-800-288-4677)

Because of the dynamic nature of the Internet, any Web addresses or links contained in this book may have changed since publication and may no longer be valid.

The views expressed in this work are solely those of the author and do not necessarily reflect the views of the publisher, and the publisher hereby disclaims any responsibility for them.

ISBN: 978-0-595-43860-0 (pbk)
ISBN: 978-0-595-60268-1 (cloth)
ISBN: 978-0-595-88184-0 (ebk)

Printed in the United States of America

For my children

Contents

Abbreviations xi
Preface xiii
Call to Duty 1
Indoctrination 11
Mine Warfare School 16
Bureau of Ordnance 23
Mousetraps 32
Noumea 50
Third Officer 64
Australia 76
New Guinea 94
Aitape 137
Command 157
Leyte 167
The Lifeboat 177
Burnout 184
Home 190
Last Days of SC 648 204
APPENDIX A   Capsules 211
APPENDIX B   Ship's Roster 221
About the Author 227

Abbreviations

AK	Cargo Ship
Apc	Coastal Transport
APD	High-Speed Transport
ARD	Floating Drydock
ASW	Anti Submarine Warfare
AWOL	Absent Without Official Leave
BM	Boatswain's Mate
BOQ	Bachelor Officers Quarters
BuORD	Bureau of Ordnance
BuPERS	Bureau of Personnel
CO	Commanding Officer
CPO	Chief Petty Officer
CV	Aircraft Carrier
CVE	Aircraft Carrier (escort)
DD	Destroyer
DE	Destroyer Escort
D-V(G)	Deck Officer, Volunteer, General
EM	Electrician's Mate
GQ	General Quarters
HMAS	His Majesty's Australian Ship
LCC	Landing Craft, Control
LCI	Landing Craft, Infantry
LCM	Landing Craft, Mechanized Equipment

LCP	Landing Craft, Personnel
LCR	Landing Craft, Rubber
LCT	Landing Craft, Tank
LCVP	Landing Craft, Vehicle-Personnel
LSD	Landing Ship, Dock
LSM	Landing Ship, Medium
LST	Landing Ship, Tank
MATS	Military Air Transport Service
ML	Motor Launch
MoMM	Motor Machinist's Mate
OD	Officer of the Deck
OPA	Office of Price Administration
OTC	Task Force Command Officer
O-V(S)	Ordnance Officer, Volunteer Specialist
PC	Submarine Chaser (173' steel-hulled)
PT	Motor Torpedo Boat
QM	Quartermaster
RAAF	Royal Australian Air Force
RADM	Rear Admiral
R&R	Rest & Relaxation
SC	Subchaser
SCTC	Subchaser Training Center
SOPA	Senior Officer Present Afloat
SS	Submarine
TNT	Trinitrotoluene, an explosive compound
USO	United Service Organization
YMS	Motor Minesweeper

Preface

This book is about my four years of active duty in the United States Naval Reserve during World War II. It is also about the U.S.S. SC 648, a United States navy subchaser, whose life as a commissioned warship paralleled mine as a commissioned officer. I served aboard SC 648 for two years. Nine months of that time I was her commanding officer.

When I reported to the ship I was probably the least qualified of any officer who ever served on a subchaser. Most subchaser officers had received ninety days of basic training and six weeks of specialized training at the Subchaser Training Center (SCTC) in Miami, Florida. I had none of that. Because of my background, I was trained to be a staff officer, not a line officer. I knew nothing about piloting, navigation, communications, engineering, radar, seamanship, ship handling, damage control, watch standing, or any of the other things so vital and routine for such duty. My job was supposed to be at a desk, not on a ship. In addition, I had a history of motion sickness ever since early childhood. A less suitable candidate for an officer on a subchaser could not have been found.

The navy didn't intend for me to serve on a subchaser. I'll take full responsibility for that. I was young, naïve, and to be truthful, quite dumb. I dreamed of being assigned to sea duty. I had the romantic notion that I should be where the action was. I was obsessed with the idea that a red blooded navy officer was supposed to be on the high seas, shooting at enemy ships and aircraft, defending the honor of his country. My ignorance and blind self-confidence were my only qualifications.

How I wangled duty aboard a subchaser and ultimately became commanding officer is included here, along with stories and pictures about where we went, some of the people encountered, plus an adventure or two.

As the smallest commissioned warship in the navy, subchasers were a breed of their own—quite different from the bigger warships that basked in their aura of spit and polish. The reader may be unfamiliar with subchasers and their role in the navy, so a brief explanation follows:

When Germany and Great Britain went to war against each other in 1939 the attacks by German U boats against British shipping were devastating. By December 1941, when we entered the war, U boats had extended their operations and were roaming the Atlantic at will, sinking merchant vessels with no regard for neutrality. They operated freely off our east coast, a coast that was (except for a few patrol aircraft) literally undefended. Merchant ships sailed unescorted, with their running lights on at night. Onshore cities blazed with lights, making it easy for the U-boats to launch torpedoes at the silhouettes. By the summer of 1942 U-boats had sunk more ships and taken more lives than we lost at Pearl Harbor..

Most American citizens were unaware of the seriousness of our situation, but our navy knew, and the U-boat menace became the navy's number one priority, even at the cost of delaying our response to the Japanese aggression in the Pacific.

The U.S. navy had been virtually destroyed at Pearl Harbor. Something had to be done quickly to stop the U-boats. Our only defense was an assortment of hastily recruited yard patrol boats (YPs), minesweepers, motor launches, sailing vessels and a "hooligan navy" of privately owned yachts and trawlers.

As early as 1939, with uncanny foresight, President Franklin D. Roosevelt had ordered the navy to design and build small vessels called "subchasers," with the ability to seek and destroy—or at least deter—enemy submarines.

Similar in general appearance to the subchasers used in World War I, there were many differences. Most of the second-generation subchasers had pre-formed cast aluminum pilot houses. For propulsion they used diesel oil instead of gasoline. They were equipped with greatly improved ordnance and more sophisticated underwater detection equipment.

Subchasers were built of wood in small, family-owned boatyards, because steel was on allocation and the big shipyards were backed up with contracts for building aircraft carriers, cruisers and destroyers. When war was declared in December, 1941, eighty 110' long subchasers were under contract in various stages of construction. By war's end, 483 wooden subchasers had been launched and commissioned.

At the outset of the war subchasers were the only waterborne means of defense against the U-boats, although everyone knew from the beginning that they were inadequate, both in size and in armament, to effectively destroy the U-boat scourge. When surfaced, a German submarine could go faster and its 4-inch guns had a much longer range than the 3-inch 50 caliber cannon or 40mm guns on the subchaser. All the U-boat had to do was get out of range and sink the subchaser with its cannon on its own terms. But the subchasers were a real nuisance to the U-boats because the U-boat was effective only when it was submerged at periscope depth, sighting and firing its torpedoes at an enemy ship.

Once a subchaser detected the presence of a U-boat with its sonar equipment, it had a big advantage. The subchaser could attack with depth charges. It could force the U-boat to stay submerged and thus drain its batteries (for oxygen supply). In this situation the U-boat would be unable to attack, rendering it powerless and allowing the convoy to proceed unharmed.

When larger ships such as destroyers and destroyer-escorts became available, the subchasers continued to escort and screen for submarines but they were no longer our first line of defense. The larger ships combined with naval airplanes to form killer groups that effectively searched and destroyed the U boats. It was in this way that the U boat threat was eliminated and the Battle of the Atlantic was won.

Throughout the war, when not engaged in escorting convoys or patrolling harbors, the subchasers were used in a variety of ways in all theaters of the war. They were ideally suited for landing control work in hundreds of amphibious landings in the European and Pacific theatres. Quiet in operation, maneuverable, and with their shallow draft, the SCs made good control boats, approaching close to the beach and guiding the landing boats. After the landing they served as a communication center for beach masters and landing control officers. In the days following the landing they would patrol the area, lay smoke screens, rescue downed pilots, ferry personnel, and perform other necessary duties. Some subchasers were equipped for shallow water minesweeping and were called upon several times to perform this highly dangerous work prior to the actual landings.

I mentioned that subchasers were the smallest commissioned warships in the United States navy. The answer to the question "Weren't PT boats smaller?" is affirmative, but PT boats were not commissioned individually. They were commissioned in squadrons.

Subchaser decks were packed with armament—a 40mm or 3" cannon forward, three 20mm AA guns aft, ASW Mousetrap projectiles, K-guns, and depth charges. Their cruising radius was 1500 nautical miles at 12K. The normal complement on a subchaser was three officers and twenty-four enlisted men, mostly reservists, unaccustomed to the rigid ways of the navy, and lacking the finer points of ship discipline and formality. Many of the officers were recent college graduates, with only ninety days of basic training and an additional sixty days of specialized training at SCTC. The "ninety-day-wonders" and their freewheeling, often scruffy-looking crews ignored many of the ways of the regulation navy and settled for their own set of rules. They were sometimes referred to as the "Donald Duck Navy" but it didn't bother them.

The cutaway illustration of a subchaser barely hints at the cramped, uncomfortable conditions for the twenty-eight men who lived aboard. The forward compartment, a space about eighteen feet long by ten feet wide, was the living quarters for sixteen men. They slept in tiered pipe bunks folded against the bulkhead when not in use. Men who wanted to sleep had to put up with others in the lighted compartment who were playing cards, talking, or, as was often the case, arguing. Eight men occupied the after crew's quarters, sharing their space with the ship's company during mess, which was prepared three times daily (when the cook wasn't seasick) in an adjoining small galley.

Subchasers, though very seaworthy, were uncomfortable even in moderate seas. The heavy roll combined with a violent pitching motion, resulted in a harsh, incessant, corkscrew pounding that permitted neither sleep nor rest for anyone. There were few creature comforts, particularly when at sea, with damp, cramped quarters, a scarcity of fresh water and palatable food. Despite the drawbacks, however, the men who served speak rather fondly of their subchaser adventures today. Most of them say they're glad they had the experience but they would never want to do it again.

Subchasers escorted hundreds of convoys, patrolled myriad harbors and picket lines. Under enemy barrage they laid smoke screens and swept mines. They rescued crashed pilots, saved drowning marines and pulled men out of waters ablaze with oil from torpedoed ships. They stood off beaches as control vessels in countless amphibious assaults (nineteen of them at Normandy alone.) Some were sunk by dive bombers and Kamikazes, others by blizzards, typhoons, and collisions. The iron men on those little wooden subchasers spilled blood on the shores of Sicily, Salerno, Anzio, and Normandy and all the way from the Solomons, New Guinea, the Gilberts and Marshalls, to the Philippines, Guam, Iwo Jima and Okinawa. By the time Germany and Japan surrendered, more than 40,000 men in 438 subchasers had fought in every theater of the war, too many never to return.

Much of this book is constructed from memory, something that plays tricks over a long period of time. I must therefore insert a disclaimer to the effect that my memory of an incident that happened over sixty years ago might disagree with another person's memory of the same incident. But the gist and the over-all picture of the incident is as real to me today as it appeared way back then.

If some of the stories may seem implausible in their specific recall of names and details, this is explained by the fact that the many letters to my parents and to my future wife, Zan, were saved. Most of them have survived sixty years of quiet storage in different dusty attics as we moved about the country. They have provided much material for recollection, including many details that normally would have been forgotten. The ship's logbook and official correspondence stored in our National Archives II facility in College Park, MD have also been invaluable. Finally, I was fortunate to have a camera while aboard the subchaser, and snapped over two hundred fifty photos. The photos displayed without credit in this book are mine. Photos from other sources are properly credited.

The reader will occasionally confront terms like "Japs" and "nigger" in conformance with the reality of that era. I implore that this offense be excused. My parents taught me never to use the word "nigger" and I obeyed. But I did say "Jap" plenty of times. Both terms are relics of the past, regrettable and best forgotten.

During the five years it took to complete this book, it turned into a family project. I'm greatly indebted to my son

Ted III for his patient assistance during the many times my computer or software failed; to my son Dan for his enthusiasm and talent for archival research; to my daughter Lucy's peerless skill as proofreader and copyeditor; to daughter Nancy's critical appraisal and suggestions, and to my son Andrew for making me a better father and a better person. Two talented friends have helped immeasurably with the cover design. Jane Schultheiss pioneered the original cover, and Matt Hirsheimer, a watercolorist and artist of note, reworked it from a photo of myself and another of the ship. The background for the frontispiece was another of Matt's efforts, in which he used a photo I snapped of our yeoman silhouetted against a sunset. Matt also constructed the maps. A last minute thanks goes to Dana Scanlon for his assistance with imaging. Lastly, I thank my loving wife, Betty, for her patience and forbearance during her many months of isolation while I wrestled with Taste of Salt.

xx   Taste of Salt

Call to Duty

On Sunday morning, December 7, 1941, I slept late, nursing a slight headache, the result of over-indulging the night before. A group of us had been whooping it up in Boston, returning to the campus quite late, feeling pretty silly. It took longer than usual to shower, shave, and get dressed. It wasn't until noon when, still somewhat groggy, I walked out the door of Gallatin Hall at Harvard Business School and started out for the dining hall. Jim McKinney fell in step with me, looking almost as bad as I felt. He had been one of the guys with me the night before. But when we entered the dining hall we were suddenly jarred into sober reality. Pearl Harbor had just had the daylights bombed out of it. Everyone was talking excitedly about it. The room was abuzz with the news.

"Those little Jap bastards!"

"How in hell do they think they can get away with it?"

"Those sons-of-bitches, they're dumber than we thought."

"We'll blow 'em away just like that."

Some of us, myself included, didn't even know where Pearl Harbor was, nor did we have any idea why we had been attacked. What we did know was that we were now at war with Japan and our immediate futures were going to be quite different than planned. Great Britain, France, and Russia were already at war with Germany and in a few days the United States would join them. With Pearl Harbor blown up, our futures were no longer hazy. Our lives would be radically different. Instead of embarking on business careers most of us would don uniforms.

Since 1939, with the beginning of war in Europe, the U.S. had remained precariously neutral. That we ultimately would be dragged into it had hovered like a dark cloud over everyone. The mood was heightened in September 1940 when Congress passed the Selective Training and Service Act requiring all men between the ages of 21 and 30 to register for the draft. Local draft boards examined your qualifications and classified you accordingly. A classification of 1-A meant you were eligible, physically and mentally, to be drafted immediately. If you could prove you were working in a job essential for national defense you stood a good chance of being deferred. Many college students with 1-A classifications were also deferred, to allow them to complete their education. Some draft boards were more stringent than others. In order to fill certain quotas, some boards drafted students right away.

I spent the remainder of that "Day of Infamy" tuned to the radio and half-heartedly dallying at my studies. Later Steve Hodges came by and we had dinner together. Steve was my best friend from boyhood. We had grown up as pals in Arlington, New Jersey, did everything together, went through high school together, and were always very close. After we graduated from high school his family moved to Toledo, Ohio, but we kept in close touch with each other. He went to Toledo U while I attended Rutgers. In the summer of 1940, when I told him I was going to go to Harvard Business School that fall, he mentioned it to his boss at the bond firm where he worked. Magnanimously, the firm encouraged him to apply, which he did, and he was accepted. The firm even helped pay some of his expenses. We were roommates that first year. You can't have it much better than to have your lifelong friend as your roommate, and the academic year 1940–1941 at the B-School was unforgettable.

Steve Hodges and the author at Harvard, April 1941

Both of us were classified 1-A but we were given deferments by our local draft boards, Steve's in Toledo, mine in Arlington. Deferments were reviewed every few months depending upon conscription needs. You couldn't count on being deferred indefinitely, but when you're young and the world is your apple you don't dwell on these things, you continue to live life as fully as possible—which is what we did.

When the first year at HBS ended in June, 1941, Steve returned to Toledo to work at the bond company that was sponsoring him. I got a summer job doing grunt work at a company in Jersey City that made tin cans. I took it partly for the experience and partly to gain credit in a second-year course at Harvard about human relations. If you wrote an acceptable paper about your summer job you'd be credited one-third of the course. It was the American Can Company and when I got home for the summer my mother told me they had phoned and wanted me to come in and fill out papers. When I entered their office and gave the receptionist my name and reason for being there, another young woman nearby turned to the half-dozen people in the office and said, in a loud voice, "He's the one from Hahvahd!" They stared at me as though I should be pitied.

I worked on the night shift in the warehouse, under the supervision of a diminutive Italian dynamo named "Lightning Joe." We loaded cases of newly made beer cans into trucks that drove across the New Jersey meadows and delivered them to the Ballantine brewery in Newark. Sometimes we went along for the ride and we were able to drink all the beer we wanted while there.

At the end of the summer I wrote a fifty-page report about the job, with descriptions of my fellow workers, their habits on and off the job, the working conditions, safety rules, ways to improve, and so on. I received an A for my efforts from my professor at Harvard. I mention this not to brag but because in my entire academic career it was unusual for me to get A's.

The downer that summer was Steve's draft board in Toledo. They wouldn't defer him any longer. In August 1941 he was ordered to report immediately for active duty in the army. If he had complied he would have been a buck private, a "grunt." Luckily, he anticipated this and had already applied to the Navy for flight training that would lead to a commission. The navy accepted him in the nick of time. That fall, instead of returning to the B-School, he was in uniform learning to be a navy pilot.

My draft board was more lenient, and granted me a deferment so I could return to Harvard for the second and final year. I took a single room in Gallatin Hall next to one occupied by Walt Guthrie, a good friend whose life, incidentally, was taken early in the war. By now the signs of our getting involved in the European war were all too evident. German U-boats were wreaking havoc within sight of our coast. There was no way the United States could remain neutral much longer. The Pearl Harbor attack settled matters. From that day forward we realized we could be called up immediately, without getting our MBA degrees. In the meantime, we could study, party, and live it up—which we did, but not in that order.

Later in the afternoon of December 7th, Steve arrived from the Squantum Naval Air Base dressed in his flying cadet's uniform. Our conversation was mostly a sober recap of our present situation and what the future might bring. He was expecting orders to Jacksonville for advanced training, and I could be drafted into the army immediately. I began considering options, one of which was to send for information about joining the Royal Canadian Air Force.

Fortunately, a more realistic option came three weeks later, when two navy officers from Boston came out to the B-School and talked to all the second-year students. They told us the Bureau of Ordnance needed men with our training for a variety of administrative jobs. They offered us commissions as OV(S) [Ordnance Volunteer Specialist] officers in the Naval Reserve. If we applied and were accepted, we could remain on inactive duty until June, thus allowing us to get our MBA degrees. We would then be called for active duty as commissioned ensigns.

The offer was tempting to those who, like me, were on the verge of getting drafted, so I signed up, along with about eighty classmates. Within a week or two we were accepted and there was no longer any mystery about our immediate future upon graduation.

That spring was filled to the brim with fleeting pleasures, our last days of academia and ivy-covered walls. Each passing week was filled with memory-laden, supremely happy days, at times tinged with guilt after reading the papers about the war. Our nights were filled with rollicking dates with girls from Wellesley and Radcliffe at places like the Café Vendome, Dinty Moore's, and Newbury Street bars, and jazz clubs. Weekends featured outings to Crane and Wingarsheek beaches with carloads of guys and their dates, plenty of beer, singing, flirting, dalliance, and more, almost within sight of (and completely ignorant of) the U-boats and the wholesale slaughter at sea. I visited Lexington to relax with my aunt and uncle and make desultory moves on a girl I imagined I loved passionately and who conveniently lived around the corner from my aunt. (The passion was unrequited, the moves rebuffed.)

Events were taking place that would impinge on me later. In Charleston (Boston) navy yard a facility for anti-submarine warfare (ASW) training began operations; in New Guinea the Japanese took over Finschhafen and Hollandia; in Miami the navy opened a training school called Subchaser Training Center (SCTC).

April 18, 1942. Leesburg, NJ. Delaware Shipbuilding Co. launches a subchaser designated SC 648.

National Archives (19LCM Box 525)

I received a letter from the navy wanting to know why I had said I was born in Arlington when my birth certificate stated I was born in Kearny. At Harvard I had gotten used to telling people I was from Arlington because I thought "Arlington" sounded classier than "Kearny." The false pride backfired and I had to write a convoluted letter explaining the difference. Vanity notwithstanding, the application was accepted without argument and on March 6, 1942, I was appointed an Ensign OV(S) in the United States Naval

Reserve, temporarily assigned to inactive duty pending completion of my studies at Harvard.

By the way, Kearny is a wonderful town full of good, solid, hardworking people of many diverse ethnic and religious origins. It lies on a red sandstone bluff overlooking the Jersey Meadows, three miles north of Newark. Across the meadows you can see the skyscrapers of Manhattan. I remember sitting in study hall at Kearny High School and daydreaming as I looked across the meadows at the outline of the skyscrapers of New York, thinking that some day I would be running a business out of one of those buildings. The Passaic River marked the western boundary of Kearny, across which sprawled the towns of Belleville, Bloomfield, Nutley, and Montclair, dotting the hills we called the Orange Mountains.

There's a popular belief that if you've gone to Harvard you've had a privileged, moneyed, comfortable life. It was definitely a privilege for me to attend Harvard Business School and I had a comfortable, happy youth. But we never had any money. When I graduated I owned one suit and was $3,000 in debt to a student loan arranged by Harvard.

My dad taught chemistry at Dickinson High School in Jersey City. At the bottom of the Great Depression his salary was cut 52 percent. For years he struggled to keep the house he had bought, but the bills for my mother's poor health and the money for my brother Dave and me to help pay our college expenses finally caught up with him. The bank foreclosed his mortgage and dad never owned a house again. It happened quietly and privately. He and Mother never told me until after they had moved into a rented house in the same neighborhood. Dad bore the pain with dignity, never complaining, and he and Mother kept their sense of humor and their good standing in the community. They were a stirring example of rock solid stability to me and to all who knew them. The rented house I came home to after graduation was small but it was neat and comfortable. Mother still played the piano, Dad avidly continued his hobbies of astronomy and photography, and I was the luckiest guy in the world to have such outstanding, loving parents.

Some eighty classmates and I, who had signed with the navy were awarded our MBA degrees late in May. All we could do now was wait for the navy to summon us for active duty. I skipped the pomp and circumstance of graduation to go home and enjoy what little precious time was left before I was called.

By now Pearl Harbor was only six months old but life for ordinary civilians had changed dramatically. Women donned hard hats and worked alongside men in plants converted to the manufacture of military goods. Gold stars began appearing in windows, signifying a son lost fighting for his country. Dad showed me his gas rationing coupons. No longer could he just jump in the car and take a trip. Instead, he had to use the car only for bare necessities—the grocery, doctors' appointments, and the like. Meat ranged from scarce to unobtainable. Instead of dairy-made butter you bought white-colored margarine and mixed it with a yellow substance to make it look like butter. Advertisements to "Buy War Bonds" were in all the newspapers. Dad volunteered as an air raid warden. Mother joined a group of church ladies making bandages and layettes. Children collected string and helped grow Victory gardens.

Mother kept me informed about high school friends who were now in the service, some of them already overseas and fighting. Too many would not return, including good high school friends like Gene Ebert, Roger Murray, and Ivor Emerson, all killed in action. My older brother Dave had moved to Wilmington, Delaware, where he worked as a chemical engineer with DuPont. His job was in a war-related activity, thus his draft status was deferred indefinitely.

There wasn't much for me to do around the house. I sensed the dread my parents felt, a cloying and unspoken feeling that made me want to be somewhere else. Most of my friends were in the service or had moved away. I spent my time helping dad with yard work, playing cards, reading, and puttering around the house. We went to the movies and saw "How Green Was My Valley" and "Citizen Kane." I secretly wished for my orders to come through.

In June they finally arrived. I was ordered to report on July 15th for "temporary active duty under instruction" at Dartmouth College, Hanover, New Hampshire. Forms were included for a physical exam, a uniform allowance, and travel expenses. Instructions told me where I could buy uniforms.

I had no money to buy either uniforms or the train fare to Hanover. As usual, long-suffering Dad came to the rescue. He accompanied me to the First National Bank to co-sign a loan of $250. We negotiated with Bob Jones, a high school classmate who worked at the bank. Years later, while attending my fiftieth high school class reunion, I met Bob again. By then he was president of the same bank. I asked him whether he remembered that loan.

The new ensign and parents, June 1942

"I sure do," he said, his eyes twinkling. "Want another one?"

A few days after receiving my orders I went over to New York to buy uniforms. The All-Bilt Uniforms store in lower Manhattan was doing a land-office business selling army and navy uniforms to thousands of recruits. Young men swarmed around the store while clerks and tailors bustled about with sales slips and measuring tapes. The clerk who waited on me was experienced, especially with green officers. After selling me a set of blues, a set of khakis, and a white dress uniform, all with the proper cap covers, bars, and epaulettes, he produced a handsome sword.

"You'll need this for dress parades," he said.

The sword looked long and ungainly. I hesitated.

"It's only $15 because with the uniform I can make it a package deal," he wheedled.

I shook my head. Something wasn't right. I couldn't picture myself wearing a sword.

He was used to refusals. "Are you reporting to a ship or will you be land-based?" he asked.

"Probably land-based," I replied.

He produced an ugly, short-handled trench spade, saying, "You'll need this when you get out on those islands. Could save your life. It's only three dollars."

I shook my head again.

"OK, here's something you're definitely going to need." He opened a green canvas collapsing bucket. "All kinds of germs in that water out there."

He finally gave up, but today I think I should have bought the sword. It would have been a nice memento of those dizzying, unfolding, uncertain days.

Indoctrination

A thousand newly commissioned navy reserve officers came to Dartmouth College that summer, destined for administrative duties in the Bureau of Ordnance, Bureau of Personnel, or the Supply Corps. They came from all parts of the country. Their ages ranged from 22 to 44 years, their ranks from ensign to lieutenant commander. They were teachers, lawyers, bankers, business executives, farmers, salesmen, engineers and students.

They stripped us of all collar pins and epaulettes, thus reducing us to equal ranks as students. We lived like college students, sharing rooms in several dormitories. I shared a room in Woodward Hall with three others, two of them B-School classmates. Our daily routine began with reveille at 5:30 a.m., then muster outside at 6:00 for a half-hour of vigorous setting-up exercises, followed by a brisk march to the dining hall for breakfast. Classes, which lasted all morning, came next, with green instructors teaching Navy Regulations, Piloting, and Rules of the Road. We had a half-hour lunch break followed by infantry drills and then two hours of required athletics. After evening meal we were supposed to study until taps at 10:15 p.m. Each of us had to stand a two-hour watch during the night. I remember standing in the hall opposite the entrance door to Woodward Hall in the wee hours of the morning, thinking about how everyone else was sleeping and I was protecting them from surprise attack. It may seem comical but the war was ubiquitous, the only thing we thought about.

July 11, 1942. Leesburg, New Jersey. U.S.S. SC 648 commissioned. Miss Garnett A. Waterman christens bow with bottle of champagne. Lt(jg) Richard P. Joy, Jr commanding officer.

We sat through lectures about dress codes, how and when to salute, navy protocol, etiquette, and terminology. We were taught that navy officers were an elite group and we should maintain traditions and behave like officers and gentlemen at all times. There would be no socializing with enlisted men. If you were late to class or muster you got extra watch duty or double calisthenics. During the second week I was chosen to be muster petty officer for a platoon. This meant that I took the roll and could mark myself on time no matter what.

A real bugler sounded the calls, giving a military air to the Dartmouth campus. At reveille there was a mad dash for the "head" to shave, wash, and dress in time for company formation outside. You had to be pushy because so many half-naked men were jostling for mirror positions. In one of the scrambles I noticed Donovan, an older officer, ignoring the mirror and basins, shaving out of a paper cup of water. Instead of lathering up he rubbed bar soap on his face. A few quick, long strokes of the razor and he was out of there while the rest of us were still jostling for position. Later that day I collared him and expressed my admiration for his efficiency. He said he had no use for anyone who picked and jabbed with his razor in little sniggling strokes. "It shows a small mind with no value for time," he declared. After that I stopped shaving in little sniggling strokes.

Donovan, incidentally, was one of those natural-born leader types with a magnetic personality. A ruddy, businesslike Irishman, he'd been in the British Army in World War I, advancing from private to major in four years and earning two decorations. After the war he emigrated to America, was naturalized, and worked his way through

Harvard Law School. He built a successful law practice in Reno and owned two cattle ranches, both left behind when he joined the navy the day after Pearl Harbor. They made him a lieutenant commander. He was older and more worldly than the rest of us. He demonstrated his leadership qualities one day when we were forming up for marching drill. Most of us former civilians were abominable marchers. We shambled along in weaving lines, out of step, each of us just careful enough to keep from being placed on report. Keeping in step and marching smartly was not something we regarded necessary for winning the war.

On that day the company commander, a bored young ensign fresh out of the Naval Academy, called out Donovan's name and ordered him to come forward.

Donovan marched up and saluted the ensign smartly.

"Donovan, muster the company and take command of the drill," the ensign ordered.

"Aye Aye, SIR!" Donovan barked, sounding just like a marine private responding to a drill sergeant.

He faced the company, paused, then shouted, "CompanEEEE!"

Quiet.

"Uh ... taayn ... SHUN!"

Shoulders snapped, chins pulled in, chests stuck out.

Pause. Quiet.

"Left ... FACE!"

Snap, snap. Pause. Quiet.

"Forward ... MARCH!"

"Hut, two, thee, fo' ... Hut, two, thee, fo' ..."

Lightning had struck. His voice and demeanor electrified the men. He was Instant Fearless Leader and Drill Sergeant all in one and we loved it. He was so good at it the ensign made him permanent march leader. By the end of the summer we were marching as smartly as the cadets at West Point.

July-August 1942. SC 648 takes shakedown cruise to Boston. Returns to New York for harbor patrol duty.

A personal milestone took place that summer. Earlier that year I was friendly with a Radcliffe girl who invited me to her parent's home in Hingham. When her mother learned I would be in Hanover that summer she gave me the name of a family friend who had moved there and was working as a dental assistant. After a couple of weeks settling into the routine at Dartmouth I looked her up. She turned out to be very attractive, with eyes that sparkled, lips that invited, and a figure that would make coveralls look sexy. She was seven years older than I, and considerably more worldly and experienced. Before the summer was over I no longer was conscientiously saving something for a wedding night in the uncertain future. The brief, torrid liaison was exceptional in that milieu because men outnumbered females five hundred to one.

A few days before our graduation ceremonies each of us received orders scattering us all over the country. My orders were to "report to the Commanding Officer, USS *Bullfinch*, Yorktown, Virginia, for temporary duty under instruction in mine warfare." What luck! Bullfinch was the name of a ship! This would be sea duty. Just what I wanted! No respectable, red-blooded navy officer shuffling papers at a desk. I'd be on the high seas on a warship!

The glow didn't last very long. I learned that USS *Bullfinch* was a ship, all right. In fact, she was a minesweeper. However, she was docked semi-permanently and being used as an administrative facility for several dormitories, classrooms, and workrooms known as the Naval Mine Warfare School. The ship's name was synonymous with the school. My secret desire for sea duty would have to wait.

Closing exercises at Dartmouth were high spirited and colorful. It was a bright, sunny day in September and dozens of townspeople watched, waving little flags, while

Donovan led the entire brigade in a marching drill. The dress parade was followed by an inspection by a high-ranking officer and several aides who walked among our lines, nodding approvingly as we stood at ramrod attention. Then, with everyone at parade rest, the high-ranking officer made a speech. No one wore swords, thus vindicating my decision not to be talked into buying one at All-Bilt Uniforms.

Mine Warfare School

After two days leave, spent with my parents in Arlington, I boarded a train in Newark bound for Richmond, Virginia. Rail was the most common form of travel because airplanes were only for important people with priority orders. The train was noisy, jammed with men in uniform. It was standing room only during the hour and a half it took to reach Philadelphia. I finally found a seat, its worn drab green velour upholstery typical of the era. I was lucky to get it because the ride to Richmond lasted most of the night. Early the next morning I transferred to a C&O train for an hour and a half ride to Williamsburg, from whence two other officers and I took a taxi for Yorktown. We thought the $3.50 fare for the 14-mile taxi ride was exorbitant but the driver didn't budge. The entire 350-mile trip from Arlington to Yorktown lasted 24 hours, not bad for those chaotic times. Passenger demand had mushroomed beyond all reason but the hard-pressed railroads handled the situation quite well.

Naval Mine Warfare School was a barbed-wire compound on the York River. It was closely guarded by a detachment of U.S. Marines. Inside the compound were several camouflaged wooden buildings used for housing, classrooms, assemblies, and a gymnasium. I was a member of a new class to be trained in mines. The training would take six weeks. In a letter home, I wrote:

> Our innerspring beds are made by colored mess boys who also shine shoes and take care of our laundry. We eat a lot of food dished out on indented metal trays. The

enlisted men and mess boys are not required to salute but the Marines do, and boy, they really give you a snappy salute, with a "Good morning, Sir!"

After a week we learned what we might end up doing in the navy. Thirteen of us were to be assigned to a group called the Advanced Base Group. Each of us would be sent to a remote base "like Iceland or an island in the Pacific" where we would establish a mine assembly line. The mines would be stored for the minelayers working the area. I figured it wouldn't be as exciting as sea duty but it was a chance to travel and see the world and it sounded better than an ordinary desk job. Besides, there were benefits. Overseas pay was 10 percent higher than that of stateside duty. An assignment outside the continental limits was credited with double time, so a year overseas was equivalent to two years in the states.

September, 1942. SC 648 arrives at Subchaser Training Center, Miami, FL.

Mine warfare training consisted of classes in Electricity, Magnetism, and Degaussing. In addition there was "lab"—a workshop—where we were given hands-on instruction in the three kinds of underwater mines then currently in use: contact, acoustic, and magnetic. We learned how mines worked and how to put them together and take them apart. Most of the instructors were articulate and capable. Our instructor in electricity had been an assistant professor of English at Yale. He was young and self-confident. The textbook was a navy manual titled Electricity. Each chapter ended with a review quiz. We progressed chapter by chapter, the instructor explaining everything step by step. There were a lot of guys in the class who, like myself, knew nothing about electricity, but there were a few graduate electrical engineers also.

One day one of the electrical engineers asked the instructor a question that went beyond what was in the manual. The instructor groped for an answer but the student wasn't satisfied. He pursued the subject and asked a follow-up question. The instructor said nothing. His face turned red. Tossing the manual onto his desk he stared at the offender and folded his arms. The room got very quiet. Then, holding up the manual, he glared at the class.
"Do you all see this book?"
Pause. Silence.
"This book has everything the navy needs you to know about electricity. Do you understand?"
Slamming the book down he folded his arms again.
Pause. Silence.
"I don't know a goddam thing about electricity."
Pause. Silence.
He picked the book up and waved it at the class.
"But I do know what's inside this goddam book."
Pause. Silence.
"And when I've finished with you you'll know what's inside this goddam book also. No more and no less."
He slammed the book down again and glared at us. The class broke into a loud round of applause. From that moment the manual's title changed from Electricity to Goddam Book and whenever anyone referred to it-—even while talking with the instructor-—it was the Goddam Book. He thought that was pretty funny too. We were drilled in Goddam Book until we knew everything in it like he said we would.

A letter home from Mine Warfare School reads: "In the past few years I have studied a wide variety of subjects: Real Estate Law, the Bible, Botany, French, Shakespeare, Industrial Management, Philosophy—and now Electricity and Degaussing. Some day I'll be very learned."

Weekends in Yorktown gave me opportunities to visit Virginia Beach, Williamsburg, and Norfolk. Gazing out at the Atlantic from Virginia Beach, I saw a large convoy of merchant ships stretched across the horizon with several destroyers and a blimp. Scouting planes were flying overhead. Though I only vaguely realized it, I was looking at a deadly serious scene in the Battle of the Atlantic. The merchant ships, looking as though they were sailing peacefully along, had recently adopted our most effective strategy against the U-boats: traveling in company with many other ships, behind a protective screen of surface escorts and aircraft. This simple tactic alone drastically reduced the loss of merchant ships from U-boat attacks.

One day we boarded a tugboat that took us down the York River to a point near Chesapeake Bay where we watched commando troops as they practiced riding into the beach in landing boats. In another area that day we saw several PT boats bouncing along at high speed, performing maneuvers. The war dominated our lives, with everyone and everything directed toward winning for America. I felt impatient because so many people were already doing something toward the war effort, while I was still observing as a student.

One weekend I went to Norfolk to visit Uncle Lawrie, my father's younger brother. Captain Lawrence P. Treadwell, a Naval Academy graduate and career officer, had retired shortly before the war, but voluntarily returned to active duty immediately after Pearl Harbor. During his career he had traveled the world and commanded several ships. He was stationed in Norfolk in charge of small craft inspection for the Fifth Naval District, a job he disliked, describing it as a "leftover given to retirees." He yearned for something more exciting. With his wife and two children he lived in a single-family house on the Norfolk Naval Base. His son Larry Jr. is now a retired navy captain himself. A couple of doors away from Lawrie lived Captain Elliot Buckmaster, who had been commanding officer of the carrier Yorktown, sunk in June from damage incurred during the Battle of Midway.

Uncle Lawrie was a handsome man, slender, tanned, with an engaging personality. He was an enthusiastic, low-handicap golfer. He loaned me a set of clubs and we played a nine-hole course on the base, with B-25 bombers taking off every few minutes and roaring only 500 feet over our heads. The distraction made a handy excuse for my rotten golf but it didn't bother Uncle Lawrie. He made almost every hole in par or better. That evening we went to the movies on the base and I sat with him in a

Capt. Lawrence P. Treadwell

section reserved for commanders and above in rank. Sunday morning he took me around the base, pointing out the seagoing yacht of Admiral Royal E. Ingersoll, commander in chief of the Atlantic Fleet, three old battleships left over from World War I, a couple of cruisers, and several destroyers.

On October 24, 1942, I received a certificate for completing the prescribed course in Mine Warfare, accompanied with orders to report on October 28 to the Bureau of Ordnance in Washington. Taking advantage of this unexpected four days of freedom, another ensign and I went out to nearby Langley Field to see whether we could scrounge a ride to New York via MATS (Military Air Transport Service). As luck would have it, we were able to get on a B-18 bomber, where we climbed into the bombardier's compartment in the forward belly of the plane. There, lying on our bellies during the two-hour flight, we enjoyed the vista below, once circling 150 feet over several ships accompanied by a patrol craft. Landing at Mitchell Field, I was home with my folks early that evening. There was a letter from Steve Hodges, who was on his way to the Pacific:

Lt. Stephen B. Hodges, Navy flyer, veteran of Guadalcanal, lifelong friend, roommate, brother-in-law.

12 October, 1942
Dear Ted:
We leave by plane this afternoon so I want to drop you a short note saying "goodbye" until we meet out there or until we are able to communicate. Wherever you go, please inquire for me if you do not know where I am, and I'll do the same for you. What a happy rendezvous you and I will hold some day. For you are unquestionably my most loved and respected friend. As ever, Steve.
P.S. Give your parents my regards—very best regards.

I was glad to hear from him but it added to my frustration because I was chafing at the bit for something real to do. It seemed as though everybody had a job except me. During the entire four days, mother was over-solicitous, hovering around and waiting on me as though nothing was too good for me. We went to church Sunday morning and once I heard her sucking in her breath holding back tears. Dad was quiet and whenever he spoke it was in a half-whisper. The war had made them worried and apprehensive, and it made me uncomfortable. As a parent of five children I now realize quite clearly the pain that parents bear when their child goes off to war.

On Sunday afternoon we drove to Newark for me to catch a train to Washington. I drove the car because we were running late and I thought I could make it faster than dad. We were almost at the station when a motorcycle cop pulled us over. I was wearing my dress blues and thought maybe he'd understand when I told him we were late for the train. But he was like a bulldog in distemper. He bawled me out loud and hard, "You were twenty miles over the speed limit. You think just because you're in a goddam uniform you can do as you please." He finally let me go without a ticket and "I won't forget your friggin' face." I was subdued and apologetic to my parents, and we got to the station just as the train was pulling in.

Bureau of Ordnance

The following day I reported to Lt (jg) G. H. Wilder at the Bureau of Ordnance. Three other officers reported with similar orders. We figured we were going to get our assignments. Wilder sat in a swivel chair between two large desks, each with a phone and several large stacks of paper. He was thin and wiry, with his hair combed straight back. He swiveled from one desk to the other, talking on a phone clamped between his shoulder and jowl, shuffling papers without stopping, like a puppeteer pulling strings from which our files dangled and danced.

He finally stopped and told us what was happening. We four officers were being ordered to get more training. The four of us were to proceed together to several different navy stations for instruction in various types of naval ordnance. We were placed on a per diem basis to receive $6.00 daily for room and board. Our first destination would be Newport, where we would learn about the ordnance used on PT boats. There would be no classrooms or teachers. We were to use our own initiative by finding people on the base from whom we could ask questions and who knew the answers. It was something like today's TV reality shows where strangers are grouped together to solve a problem. The only difference was the reward. Instead of cash, the winner would be better prepared to survive the war.

We found Newport swarming with uniformed people, mostly navy and mostly very boisterous. A fog had settled over the city and the glow from the street lamps over hundreds of sailors milling around on cobblestone streets outside the many bars and taverns made it look like a scene from a Charles Dickens novel. No rooms were available anywhere so we stayed in an Army-Navy YMCA, where the charge was 75¢ per night. My room was a cubicle seven by nine feet small. It was the last room at the end of a long hall so it was the last room to get steam and it was always cold. The floor below had been improvised into a ballroom for nightly U.S.O. (United Service Organization) dances. The big-beat band music reverberated throughout the building. A CPO (Chief Petty Officer) occupied the room next to mine. Every night he came in late, roaring drunk, making a loud ruckus. Fights broke out frequently, lasting hours. Each room was equipped with a loud buzzer for wake-up calls. Easily heard through the paper-thin walls, the first calls began at 5:00 a.m. and continued every fifteen minutes, jarring the last vestiges of sleep.

We were in Newport for two weeks. I make it sound pretty awful but (except for the lack of sleep) we had a pretty good time. Days were spent at the navy base, where veteran chief gunner's mates instructed us in small arms, including the Colt .45 automatic pistol, Smith & Wesson .38 caliber revolver, and Thompson submachine gun. We learned how to fire, dismantle, clean, and reassemble these weapons, and in the process acquired plenty of respect for the CPOs teaching us. We were also instructed on 20 mm Oerlikon anti-aircraft-guns, the Browning .50 caliber automatic machine gun, smoke generators, and gas masks. At a firing range at Price's Neck we fired the guns into the sky over the Atlantic. One day we joined a group of officers training for duty on PT boats and had noon chow with them. Jack Kennedy could have been one of them. We sat at the same table with Lt. Comdrs. Bulkley and Kelley of PT boat fame. They were back from the Pacific on temporary assignment to help organize a new PT squadron. Cmdr. Bulkley was famous for having ferried General MacArthur and his family off Corregidor Island during the final hours when the Philippines fell into the hands of the Japanese.

November 15, 1942. Key West, Florida. SC 648 dry-docked

Some days while we were in Newport we'd finish early and go see the local sights, including the famous Cliff Walk, a walking trail overlooking the coast. We viewed the big mansions with their spacious grounds, once occupied by industrial barons like Vanderbilt, Harriman, Colt, and Astor. Some nights we went to see movies like Bambi and The Magnificent Ambersons.

"We" consisted of the three other officers whom Lt. Wilder had assigned to this training, and me. One of the officers, Ed Guerin, was the scion of an old textile family in Woonsocket. Ed had been reared in comfortable circumstances. He understood and appreciated the good life. Every night we'd go to a fancy French restaurant that he knew. He'd be in his element. He spoke French fluently and carried on long conversations in French with the waiter while choosing the right wine for our table. He was so good at selecting foods we began letting him order the entire meal for us. One night he arranged for us to have dinner at his mother's home in Woonsocket. It was a huge mansion with a circular driveway and big carved door that was opened by a butler. We were ushered into a large foyer with a high ceiling, crystal chandelier, and chestnut woodwork. The rooms were beautifully appointed. Ed's mother, a slim, dignified lady with an accent, sat at the head of the table in the formal dining room. Two maids waited on us. I had never experienced anything like this. It was like a Hollywood movie setting.

Though I knew Ed Guerin for only a short time I've always remembered him for his grace, great sense of humor, and story-telling abilities. Thirty years later when I happened to be in Providence on business I looked him up and we had dinner together. By then he was CEO of a textile company but he hadn't changed one whit. He told stories, ordered the wine and the food, and talked to the waiters in French just like always.

We finally returned to the Bureau of Ordnance, where Lt. Wilder was still swiveling between desks, juggling papers, and talking on his shoulder phone, all at the same time. He gave us a set of new orders for "further training in ordnance." This time it was to Virginia Beach, where we were to observe various wartime training activities. After checking in the next day at the New Waverly, a beachfront hotel, we began our "training." A navy bus picked us up and took us across Cape Henry to a Section Base at Little Creek, out of which subchasers and patrol craft were operating. Nearby was an amphibious school for training in the use of landing craft and beachhead tactics. Another activity was an Armed Guard school where officers and gun crews assigned to merchant vessels were trained in defense against submarines. We didn't have a guide or instructor, we simply relied upon our own initiative to get "trained." We were to ask questions and learn as much as we could by observation. It was very frustrating. Here we were, surrounded by people busy in their war roles, while we stood by gawking and asking questions like sightseeing tourists.

Some army guys offered us a ride in a medium-sized General Grant tank, the type carried by landing craft to invasion beaches. They were good guys, except that they turned out to be con men. The four of us were crammed inside a space designed for two, directly under the turret. The crewmen wore helmets with ear protectors and facemasks but they didn't give us any. When the tank started moving the air inside the turret filled with smoke from the exhaust, nearly choking us. The noise from the engine was deafening and when they fired the cannon it felt as though our eardrums had been punctured. The driver went through some unscheduled maneuvers ("for our benefit," he later explained), tossing us back and forth unmercifully. The ride lasted only ten minutes but it was incredibly tortuous. Their fun at our expense was laughable but the experience taught me never to badmouth anyone who saw service in an army tank.

It was around this time that I began corresponding with Zan Ward, a girl I had met while hitchhiking across the country in the summer of 1940. Her real name was Elizabeth Ann Ward but her family called her Lizann. I didn't favor that nickname so I shortened it to Zan. She lived in Toledo and I had met her through Steve when she was still in high school. She was the daughter of one of Steve's bosses, a partner in a municipal bond firm. By now she was a freshman at Oberlin College. I can't recall how we got started writing back and forth but I had always stayed in touch with the Ward family. Her brother John was at M.I.T. when Steve and I were at Harvard. It just seemed natural for Zan and me to correspond in a friendly way, each of us describing what we were doing. I wrote to her from Virgina Beach:

> The sunrises here are rivaled only by the sunsets at Lake Erie. Have been getting up a half hour earlier to enjoy same. Beautiful pastel shades extending across the ocean every morning. We are staying right on the ocean at a beautiful beach with weather almost warm enough for swimming.

She replied with descriptions of life at Oberlin, weekends at home, news about her pet dog, etc. Her letters were well written and interesting, and I enjoyed the correspondence.

After a week at Virginia Beach we returned to Washington to report to Lt. Wilder and receive new orders. This time he sent us to the Charleston, South Carolina, Navy Yard for more "ordnance training," a now familiar routine that made us feel more like outcasts than naval officers. It was as though the navy was hard pressed to find something for us to do. We were feeling unnecessary and unwanted.

Elizabeth Ann Ward

In Charleston Ed Guerin and I shared a room on the third floor of one of Charleston's old homes. It had tall white columns facing the Ashley River and was owned by a cotton broker. Every morning an officers' bus picked us up and took us to the base three miles away. We donned work clothing and roamed the seventeen square miles of navy yard in little trains left over from the 1939 New York World's Fair. Our roaming was unsupervised, at will, poking into machine shops, a foundry, a sheet metal shop, and galvanizing, pre-fabrication, boiler, pipe bending, welding, and fitting-out shops. We watched giant cranes lifting tons of steel and then dropping them with lots of noise. We talked with British, Norwegian, and Dutch officers and sailors, old-time machinists, helpers, pretty waitresses, and grizzled chief petty officers. We stared at ships under repair, listened to riveting, banging, compressed air hissing, and whistles blowing. We followed our orders to the letter, and our morale was zero. We watched an expert working on a torpedo and got him to explain some of its secrets, none of which we remembered. A British trawler at dockside was undergoing a conversion to minesweeping duty. A crisp, young British officer with a strong, clipped accent gave us a tour of his minesweeper. He pointed out the features of the ship with pride, although sometimes his accent was hard to understand. At one point he said, "Y'know, we have all Scots and Injuns aboard."

"Is that so?" we replied politely, looking around for distinguishing ethnic features among the crew but seeing only rather ordinary cockney seamen.

Later we learned he had said, "We have Hall-Scott engines aboard."

Ed Guerin said Charleston reminded him of northern France, with its narrow cobblestone streets, stuccoed houses, fancy iron grillwork, high walls, and gates behind which were gardens blooming with poinsettias and camellias. Charleston streets had British names like Limehouse, Lamboll, Meeting, King, and Queen and were lined with palm trees. People spoke with genteel accents. But there was another side to Charleston. Outside the old, dignified area of beautiful homes and mansions lay block after block of dingy unpainted shacks, the dwellings of 40,000 black people. I was told the white, aristocratic homeowners were unshaken by this and considered it a part of the quaintness and individualism of the city.

Charleston is the home of The Citadel, the Military College of South Carolina. When we walked around the city, especially in the late afternoon and early evening, cadets in uniform would be walking about also, in pairs or in groups. When they passed us they would salute smartly and we, of course, returned the salute. One early evening we were strolling about old Charleston. We kept meeting so many cadets the saluting got tiresome so I decided to ignore them. We passed one group of three without incident and then passed a second group of four. Just as I was beginning to think it was OK to ignore them I felt a tap on my shoulder.

"Sir, I passed you just now and you didn't acknowledge my salute, sir." The cadet eyed me questioningly.

"I beg your pardon," I said, briskly saluting.

"Thank you, sir," he said. He returned the salute and rejoined his pals.

One evening we went to a concert of the Fish Jubilee Singers at the Morris Street Baptist Church. Behind the altar was a giant painting of the River Jordan. We were the only white people there. We sat in the rear and listened to a really good program of spirituals and sacred songs. The music was beautiful and inspiring. A young black man got up and, after praising the singers in a very cultured voice, pointed to us in the rear and welcomed us as their guests, adding, "We want you to feel at home here."

On our way back from Charleston we stopped in Norfolk. I took the three officers to Uncle Lawrie's office so they could say they shook hands with a real navy captain. Then we went to Yorktown for a quick ho-hum review of the Mine Warfare School. From there we went back to Washington and the Bureau of Ordnance.

> *December 7, 1942. Aboard SC 648 at Key West, Florida. Lt(jg) Richard P. Joy relieved of command by Lt(jg) Donald H. Lescohier.*
> *December 9, 1942. In company with three other subchasers, SC 648 escorts convoy to New Orleans.*
> *December 17, 1942. SC 648 escorts convoy to Key West,*

It was a week before Christmas. A whole year had gone by since the attack on Pearl Harbor and we were still unemployed and feeling as useless as warts. Rail travel was slow, overcrowded and hectic. It was very difficult to make connections and room reservations. You couldn't plan ahead because orders would change. Whenever I got to Union Station knowing I had to stay overnight, I had a routine for finding a hotel room. I'd join a line waiting for a phone booth, making sure it was one that had a phone book. Sometimes it took an hour's wait. Finally inside the booth I'd look up hotel listings in the yellow pages and call one after another to find a room, a bed, a cot. Once I waited an hour for a booth and when I finally got inside I discovered the hotel listings had been ripped out. I stayed in the booth anyway, inventing likely names for hotels and looking for them in the white pages. I found one named the New Colonial and they offered to put a cot in a janitor's maintenance room for me. I accepted and it turned out pretty well because they paid for my breakfast the next morning. You couldn't be fussy. Sometimes you doubled up and shared a room with total strangers. One night I was booked into a room with an army private and his bride. They'd been married only a few hours. They shared a bed on one side of the room while I slept in a cot on the other side. They made love all night and their groaning and moaning made sleep impossible.

Mousetraps

Christmas arrived and the war hung over everyone like a cloud. I had four days of leave and came home knowing it was probably the last time for a while. Mother and Dad showed their anxiety but we made the best of it. Brother Dave was married and working as a plant manager for DuPont in St. Paul. Mother made some of my favorite dishes (Boston baked beans, rhubarb pie), we had visits with friends, played cards, and talked about the times—the rationing, the price controls, the blackouts, the draft, and the progress of the war.

Off the coast the U-boats were still wreaking havoc. U.S. forces had landed at Casablanca. The Japanese had taken over most of Melanesia. The navy fought big battles—Java Sea, Coral Sea, Midway, Savo Island, and others. Guadalcanal was synonymous for jungle fighting, malaria, and the U.S. Marines. Steve was there. The war was on everyone's mind.

The day after Christmas I received a phone call from Lieut. Wilder telling me to report back right away because "something was up." An hour later I was on my way, after a poignant leave-taking with Dad and Mother.

The next morning, while walking down the hall to Wilder's office, I fell in step with Carrol "Cal" Miller, a lieutenant (jg) and fellow ordnance student who had been with another group of observers similar to mine. He was from Pittsburgh and newly married. He had received the same urgent phone call from Wilder. When we entered and Wilder spotted us he stopped swiveling and paper shuffling and told the yeoman to hold the phone calls.

"Well, guys," he said, "It looks like we've got something you can sink your teeth into. We've picked you both for jobs."

He told us about a weapon newly developed for fighting submarines. The official term for it was the ASW Projector Mark 20, but it went by the nickname "Mousetrap." Forty sets of Mousetraps were being shipped to the European theater and forty sets to the Pacific theater. They needed to be installed on subchasers and patrol craft in both theaters. Because Mousetraps were new and no one knew about them, Miller and I were to be sent out to supervise their installation and instruct the subchaser crews in their proper use. One of us would go to Europe and the other to the Pacific. It was a top-secret project and Wilder impressed upon us the importance of keeping it that way.

The first step was to learn everything we could about Mousetraps and about antisubmarine warfare in general. We would first go to Boston for ten days at the ASW (Antisubmarine Warfare School), then to SCTC (Subchaser Training Center) in Miami to observe how they were installed on subchasers, and finally to Key West to watch them being fired at sea from a subchaser. Wilder then gave us each a packet of papers to study. They contained a quick review of antisubmarine warfare and more top-secret information about Mousetraps.

With the exception of more sophisticated tracking gear, the procedure for fighting submarines had not changed much from World War I. The depth charge was the principal weapon, an "ash can" containing 300 pounds of granular TNT that could be set to explode at different depths by means of a pistol/booster assembly. Depth charges were rolled off racks at the stern and could also be propelled from port and starboard sides by means of a device called a K-gun. In a standard attack, after determining the bearing, speed, and depth of the submerged submarine by means of sonar-echoing, the attack vessel would bring its heading to a course and speed designed to place it in position for dropping depth charges, assuming the sub remained on its determined course and speed. The charges were dropped and launched in a pattern calculated to surround the target with lethal explosions.

Several variables made an ideal attack difficult. The submarine could quickly change its depth, stop moving, or change or reverse course. As the attack vessel drew closer to the target the sonar's ping and its echo merged into a single sustained sound, causing uncertainty for the attacking vessel. Often the contact would be lost. This provided a margin of safety for the enemy. The attack vessel was irreversibly dedicated to a course and speed calculated to intersect the target. But because depth charges were mounted on the stern of the subchaser it meant having to reach, then pass over a point where the submarine's estimated course and speed would intersect it, before dropping. If the calculations were accurate the submarine would be hit and sunk, but the lapse of several seconds gave the enemy time to maneuver itself out of danger.

Mousetraps would overcome this critical loss of time by projecting smaller, rocket-type depth charges ahead of the attacking vessel. Mousetrap charges required no last-minute depth settings and were designed to explode only on contact. If no explosions were heard, there was no hit. After firing the Mousetraps the attacking vessel would normally continue, launching "ash cans" in the conventional manner. The Mousetrap attack preceded the depth charge attack much as a boxer makes a left jab before delivering the knockout blow with his right.

At the conclusion of Wilder's briefing, orders were drawn up and Cal and I boarded a train for Boston that afternoon. This turn of affairs was exhilarating. I would finally be doing something useful in the war effort. Also, I'd be going overseas.

The Boston ASW School was on the second floor of a ramshackle building in the Charleston Navy Yard. We stood in a room fitted out to look like a ship's bridge, complete with binnacle, wheel, engine controls, rangefinder, and even a pair of binoculars for realism. Nearby was a chart table for plotting bearings and fixes, and off to one side was a console operated by a sonarman also in training. The console replicated the sound of pings and their resulting echoes, similar to those in a real attack. The sonarman would announce a hypothetical contact with a submarine and we'd "attack" with a run on the target, ordering the "wheel" and "engine room" to change bearings and speeds according to the information relayed from the sonarman. At what we believed to be the correct moment we'd give the order to drop depth charges.

The instructors sat in an adjoining room with a simulated tracking device that projected progress of the attack on a screen, showing mockups of the ship and the submarine maneuvering, one to kill, the other to avoid being killed. When the depth charges "detonated" a red flash appeared on the screen. If the flash occurred near or on the submarine the attack was judged successful. It took lots of practice because the instructors maneuvered the target every which way. We made many runs to become even partially proficient. Compared with today's highly sophisticated video games it was very crude, although it seemed fascinating and marvelous to us at the time.

During our stay in Boston I attended a New Year's party with several B-School classmates and had a couple of visits with Aunt Bertha and Uncle Morris. At the end of ASW training we took a train back to Washington, then to Miami, where on January 18th we reported to SCTC. It was the first time I had ever been that far south and the difference in the weather when we alighted was startling. Miami was bathed in brilliant sunshine and in our blues it was as though we had stepped into a sauna.

January 6, 1943. SC 648 escorts convoy to Guantanamo Bay,Cuba.
January 11, 1943. SC returns to Key West.

> *January 19, 1943. SC 648 sails to Miami. Weather bad, seas heavy. Ship almost broaches.*
> *January 23, 1943. Lt(jg) Donald H. Lescohier relieved of command by Lt(jg) Paul Allen Spaugh. Drydocked for ordnance changes. 3"50 caliber gun replaced by 40mm Bofors anti-aircraft gun. Mousetrap rails and projectiles installed.*

Miami swarmed with men in uniform and most of the hotels had been taken over by the army or navy. Drill formations of marching men passed by everywhere. The air was charged with a spirit of patriotism and no matter where you were or where you looked, America was on a mission and there was no question about the country being at war.

We booked into the Liberty Hotel on Fourth Street, then went over to Miami Beach where, except for the presence of so many uniforms, there was everything a resort could offer—nightclubs, dance bands, sightseeing cruises, yacht basins, no food shortages—a veritable playground. At the Park Avenue Restaurant, where we dined on frogs' legs, someone pointed out Leon Henderson of the O.P.A. (Office of Price Administration). We also saw "Johnny" of the Philip Morris radio program, a short-statured person well known for his commercial, a long, drawn-out "Caaaawwll for Philip Morrrrrrrrris!" He wore his bellboy uniform and people hounded him for autographs.

At SCTC the next morning we went aboard a subchaser tied up at the dock and studied how the Mousetrap rails were installed (they had to be at just the right angle) and how the projectiles were stored. (The subchaser might have been SC 648, though there's no way of knowing for sure.) The Mousetrap installation was simple and straightforward and we were able to board a bus for Key West that afternoon. Before leaving we picked up a message from Lt. Wilder informing us that Cal and I would both go to the South Pacific while another team was being prepared for

Europe. We also picked up mail at SCTC, including a letter from Steve in Guadalcanal:

> We have developed a new standard of value out here. Among our highest pleasures is a cup of cold, clear water. At this spot the water is good so we are lucky. As we fill a cup we look at it affectionately and think of what it means to men. Don't gulp it down. The ecstatic thrill of gulping water is too short-lived. Drink it in even mouthfuls and come to enjoy between each swallow.
>
> Wood means so much more to us now. A solid piece of ¾" pine makes a dry, warm footing when we get out of our cots in the morning. It's good footing too for our bucket shower. It keeps us out of the mud. An undamaged fruit box makes a fine bookshelf or clothing locker. Next time you see a clean cut piece of pine board give it a kindly pat and say, 'You're a good thing. People should love you more".... Please inquire for me wherever you go, particularly in the Pacific area. I'll do the same for you. Gosh! But it will be swell to see you. As ever, Steve

The bus ride to Key West provided spectacular views from the long causeway crossing the Keys. Looking down from high above the clear, turquoise blue water we saw manta rays, large fish, and a shark here and there. We arrived in blistering heat late in the afternoon and found the same shortage of rooms as everywhere else. We finally found the Hotel La Concha off Duval Street. It looked all right from the outside but inside it was dirty and dumpy with a tiny room, no bath, and no air conditioning. We had no choice but to take it. On the way back from dinner we bought a bottle of rum and some Cokes. Cal spotted a good-sized coconut lying on the ground and brought it back to the room. The ice machine was broken so we poured ourselves warm drinks and relaxed.

Cal and I knew each other quite well by now and were good friends. He was thin and wiry, with Irish blue eyes and a very quick wit. He was a couple of years older than I and, having recently married and left his new bride in Pittsburgh, didn't relish the thought of going overseas. The heat in the room was oppressive. We stripped to our shorts, sipped our drinks and made small talk. Cal was curious about the coconut.

"Wonder how they open these things," he mused.

He fished in his suitcase for a small hunting knife. The blade was dull. Between sips he began jabbing the husk, supporting it between his legs. The husk was tough, resistant. "Jeez, this is tough," he muttered. A small piece came off.

"Hey, now you're getting it!" I encouraged. He jabbed some more. "Have another drink, you need some strength." He sat down on the floor and began hacking and cutting in earnest. The coconut resisted. It became a wrestling match and the husk showed signs of winning.

"Whew!" He leaned back, sweat pouring off his arms and chest.

"Stoke up," I suggested..

He took a long swallow from his glass.

"Ever drink coconut milk fresh from the shell?" he asked.

"No, I can't wait."

He tussled and jabbed, making progress. After several more minutes, the outer husk was off and the coconut lay bare. By now Cal was sweating like a pig. He sat on the floor, lit a cigarette, and took another long swallow of rum and coke.

"Hey, hey!" I cheered, raising my glass to him.

"Yeah, now to get inside it. You still want a taste of milk, right?" He stabbed at the coconut. It rolled across the floor. He got up from the floor and started dressing.

"Where you going?" I asked.

"Gotta get something to bang with."

"Boy, you got it bad."

He went out and returned with a brick.

"This precious milk better be worth it," I commented.

Holding the knife point against the coconut he banged the other end of the knife with the brick. "Ouff!" The coconut slipped and rolled across the room. Blood oozed from his hand. I helped with some bandages from my toilet kit.

"Wait till morning, you'll feel better." I suggested

"You kidding?" He was like one possessed. After a few more jabs he finally got through. He held a glass to it and poured out an inch of cloudy liquid. Crumbs of husk floated in it. He raised it up.

"Heil Hitler, you bastard," he said, taking a sip.

He held it out for me.

"Heil Hitler, you bastard," I said, finishing it off.

That was the extent of our binge in Key West. At 6:00 a.m., groggy, we made our way to the pier and waited to board a subchaser for a day of Mousetrap trials. It may have been SC 449, a subchaser that served most of the war as a training vessel at the Sound School. Diesel fumes assaulted our nostrils, mingled in the heavy mist. On the flying bridge the captain, a lean lieutenant (jg), beckoned us to come aboard. The deck was cluttered with ammo boxes, hatches, goosenecks, toolboxes, gun platforms, davits, a wherry, depth charge racks, and other gear. Six enlisted men joined us as passengers. They were future sonar operators who had come along to practice operating the sonar gear and learn some finer points of ASW.

The diesel fumes were inescapable. I thought of my boyhood motion sickness and wondered whether I'd be seasick. A letter home answers that question:

> The first day I lost my breakfast but not my lunch. This was because I didn't eat any lunch. The second day I only lost the orange juice of my breakfast because that's all I had for breakfast. I was able to eat lunch without losing it. Lunch consisted of two saltines.

The two days of practice were blessed with relatively smooth seas. A submerged friendly submarine served as the target and we practiced attacks just as in ASW School in Boston, only this was more realistic. We made one test firing and when the two days were up we felt quite familiar with the Mousetrap.

> *February 4, 1943. SC 648 departs Miami in company with nine other subchasers. Arrives at Coco Solo Submarine Base, Panama.*

On February 4, having received our orders to report to the Commander Naval Bases, South Pacific Area, for duty, Cal and I boarded a train for the three-day trip across the continent. The train, emblazoned "The Portland Rose—A Triumph in Train Comfort," was crammed with soldiers, sailors, marines, and officers of all ranks. As officers, Cal and I enjoyed the luxury of berths, while enlisted men had to make do in their coach seats. The train stopped several times to allow us to get out and stretch our legs. At each stop there were women serving coffee and doughnuts. Everyone waved the two-fingered Victory sign at us. In Chicago I bought a waterproof wrist-watch for $22.50. I wrote to Zan:

> We are crossing Salt Lake. I sit and take stock of things, the past and the future. It's hard to say what it adds up to. I wonder about the test of fear and how I will react to it. I enjoy your letters because they are fresh and spontaneous and I hope you will continue to write. Now that you are in college you are doing something worthwhile and wonderful and it makes me realize even more why we're fighting this war.

A navy commander by the name of Sheridan was on the train with us. He cut quite a figure. He was an extrovert who talked with everyone. He sported a flowing mustache, a goatee, a bashed-in nose, and a cauliflower ear. He told me he had been around the world seven times. He knew my uncle Lawrie in Norfolk. A mustang (career officer who comes up through the ranks), he was on his way to join a ship somewhere in the Pacific. On the train also was a garrulous Australian general. He and Commander Sheridan struck up a convivial acquaintance. At one of our stops the two went into a coffee shop across the tracks. Dressed in full uniforms with medals and ribbons on their chests, they looked impressive. A middle-aged woman behind the counter stood with her hands on her hips studying them. Looking straight at Sheridan but pointing at the Australian's brass hat, she said, "Well, I know you're a Russian general, but who's that guy?." "He's my valet," the commander replied, without missing a beat

San Francisco was bustling with people on the move, many of them in uniform. The navy placed us on wait status for overseas transportation. The waiting time would be anywhere from two days to two weeks. We booked rooms at the Whitcomb Hotel near the Civic Center and hunkered down in search of pleasures typical of the time, which were to "eat, drink, and be merry, for tomorrow we die." We were there for a dizzying ten days and lived it up, doing everything from sightseeing and visiting classy places like the Top of the Mark to pub-crawling in sleazy dives on Market Street. I renewed my love affair with that great city that had begun two years earlier when I was hitchhiking around the country.

February 13, 1943. SC 648 transits Panama Canal, moors at Balboa, Canal Zone.

The call finally came, and on February 15th we boarded the USS *Rixey*, bound for Noumea, New Caledonia, in the South Pacific. She was a 22,000-ton cargo vessel that had been converted into a hospital ship. She was crammed with sick bays, hospital equipment, doctors and nurses, an impressive concentration of medical facility and talent. Some of the doctors would distinguish themselves during the war by discovering new ways for treating trauma. Others would never return. They were from all over the United States and included every specialty and skill for treating the human body and every possible disease or condition. An entire company of marines and numerous other uniforms from the army, navy, and Marine Corps rode as passengers. There were many officers, all with their orders and destinations, all with one common purpose.

From San Francisco we stopped at San Diego to take on more personnel, giving Cal and me a chance to make a hurried excursion to the famous San Diego Zoo. By early evening we were once again underway. The ship took the southerly route, which was deemed safer. The crossing took twenty-two days. During the entire voyage the weather was calm and the seas were placid. Everyone was pretty much relaxed. Had it not been for the war and the grim purpose of the voyage, it could almost have been a pleasure cruise. We watched porpoises swimming playfully alongside the bow, their glistening black bodies gracefully swooping up and down through the dark blue water. Flying fish sprang out from the sides of the ship, sailing just above the surface fifty yards or more, a marvel of curious behavior. At night the blacked-out ship was mysterious and alone on the vast, calm Pacific. These were the times I often went topsides and lay on my back, gazing in wonderment at the immense sky with its Milky Way and multitudinous stars. It was a dreamy, peaceful interlude, a momentary escape from the reality that lay ahead.

February 18, 1943. SC 648 departs Balboa, Canal Zone in company with a large convoy of subchasers and minesweepers with U.S.S. Pecos, a navy oiler, acting as mother ship. Destination: South Pacific.

The *Rixey* stopped for three days at Pango Pango (now spelled Pago Pago) on the island of Tutuila in American Samoa. This is the island where the old movies "Hurricane" and "Rain" were filmed and where Dorothy Lamour made the sarong famous. The ship anchored in a little cove amid beautiful tropical surroundings and some of us were able to go ashore for a few hours. The natives were handsome, friendly, and intelligent. There was a row of small shops where you could buy beads made from seeds, grass skirts, and native carvings. I tried bargaining for a grass skirt but the old woman wanted $5.00, which I thought was extravagant. I had lunch with Dick Simpson, a Harvard classmate stationed on Tutuila.

My berth on the *Rixey* was the top one of a triple-tiered bunk. Twenty inches separated me from the overhead (ceiling). The tier was mounted against a steel bulkhead, on the opposite side of which were the galley ranges. The galley was in constant use during the day, raising the temperature around the bunk to 120 degrees. It was so hot it was impossible to take a nap. At night it cooled down somewhat, but as we neared the equator it got worse. My sheets were soaked with perspiration and I slept in a slosh of sweaty wetness.

Another inconvenience was a sinus headache that got so nagging and persistent it made me feel sick. There were lots of good doctors and sick bays aboard so I sought treatment from an ear-nose-throat doctor who was filling in while traveling as a passenger. When his medications proved useless he decided to flush my sinuses out. I sat in a chair like a dentist's chair and he tied a plastic sheet around my neck. Standing behind the chair he inserted a U shaped metal tube up my nostril. The tube was connected to a hose through which he sloshed warm water up and around in my nose. It had no effect, the sinuses still wouldn't unclog. After a minute of this he said, "Hold tight, you might feel something." He pressed the tube up, hard against the bony structure of the sinus. Suddenly my head imploded. With a grating crunch he broke through a bone into the sinus cavity. Warm water gushed into the cavity as though a dam had burst. A big gob of yellow mucus swirled into the spittoon I was holding. Relief was instantaneous. A few minutes later I walked out with my head clearer than it had felt in many months and it stayed that way for years. Nose doctors don't do that now, at least that's what my current nose doctor tells me. He says what the doctor did to me on the *Rixey* was about as primitive as when they used leeches in the Middle Ages. But sometimes when my sinuses get blocked I think wistfully about that *Rixey* doctor.

February 25, 1943. SC 648 and convoy cross Equator.

March 1, 1943. SC 648 General Quarters. Possible submarine attack. Proved false.

March 10, 1943 SC 648 and convoy arrive Bora Bora.

On March 11 the *Rixey* finally arrived at Noumea, the capital city of New Caledonia, a cigar-shaped island eight hundred miles east of Australia. A French Territory, it was the headquarters for the Fifth Fleet under the command of Admiral William F. "Bull" Halsey.

When we disembarked from the *Rixey* I was thinking I must have lost ten pounds during the crossing because of all the sweating in that hot bunk. A short drive in a jeep took us to the Advanced Naval Base, a group of Quonset huts used for offices and living quarters. A hut with flowers in front and a sign that read "Commanding Officer, Captain R. H. Henkle" was where we were to report. H-hour for our destiny with Mousetraps, our "top secret mission," had arrived.

A yeoman at the front desk took our orders into Captain Henkle's office. A few minutes later we were ushered in. The captain, a red-faced, unpleasant-looking man in his mid-50s, sat behind his desk reading the orders and frowning. He didn't bother to look up, and we stood waiting. He kept scowling. Finally he looked at us.

"Well," he said, "I'm looking at these orders and they don't tell me a damn thing. What brings you two here?"

We had agreed beforehand that Cal would do the talking. He explained to the captain how we had been sent by the Bureau of Ordnance to supervise the installation of Mousetraps on patrol craft and subchasers operating in the area.

Captain Henkle looked puzzled. "Mousetraps? What the hell are Mousetraps?" he asked.

Cal began explaining. The captain interrupted. "You mean those rocket charges you shoot from the bow?"

"Yes, sir," said Cal.

"And you say you're here to install them?"

"Yes, sir."

"Wait a minute," the captain said, reaching for a phone and dialing. "If this is what I think it is ..." Someone on the other end answered.

"Chief? Captain Henkle here. Tell me, what's the story on those rails, those projectors they shipped in? I think they're called Mousetraps." He listened, scowling, phone pressed to his ear. The room felt warm. Cal's forehead was glistening. My palms were beginning to sweat.

"Well, are they using them?" Pause.

"You mean they're installed and working?" Pause.

"Any problems?" Pause.

"Thanks, chief, that's all."

The captain hung up the phone, leaned back in his chair and looked at us hard. He picked up the orders and read them again.

"Son-of-a-bitch," he said, slow and soft, glowering. He was like a tiger switching his tail. My kidneys were beginning to throb. I wanted to pee. The captain shook his head slowly. He looked at Cal.

"You say you were sent out here to supervise these things?"

"Yes, sir."

His face was very red. "The chief tells me they're on the ships and they're working fine. Tell me something, Lieutenant—what's-your-name—Miller? How long have you been in the navy?"

"A year and a half, sir."

"And you, Treadwell, how long have you been in the navy?"

"About the same, sir, a little less."

"Have either of you been on a ship or had sea duty?"

"No, sir," in unison.

"Either of you know anything about ships?"

"Not really, sir," Cal said.

"What do you know?"

Cal shifted, perspiration in big beads on his forehead. He began to speak but the captain raised his hand. "Wait," he said, looking straight at me, "Ensign, you say you've been over a year in the navy. You must know something. Tell me what you've learned since you've been in the navy."

My mouth felt dry, my kidneys throbbed, and my palms were sweating. "Uh, sir, we know the Mousetraps pretty well and I was at Mine Warfare School and learned quite a bit about mines and before that I was at Indoctrination School and ..."

He interrupted. His face was purple.

"Ensign, you don't know shit from shinola! Jud, can you come in here?"

Henkle's executive officer, a three-striper, entered from an adjacent office. Short and trim, his face was a pallid yellow color. I learned later he was suffering from dengue fever. He had been on the carrier Yorktown, which had been sunk in the Battle of Midway.

The captain handed our orders to him. "Jud, look at this from BuPers. They keep sending these know-nothings out here and they expect us to take care of them. What in

Christ's name are they thinking of? We've got too many people who don't know anything. We don't need any more. This is the third pair to come in here in a week and I'm getting fed up. They think they can run the war from Washington and they don't know a goddam thing."

The exec scanned our orders, then looked up. The two of them looked at us as though we were rotting cabbage. I couldn't believe what was happening. Cal's face was grayish white. His face dripped with sweat. My shirt was drenched.

The captain said, "All right, I know what I'm going to do with you two. Maybe it'll stop all this. I'm going to make an example of you two. I'm going to send both of you back to Washington and let them figure out what to do with you. We're fighting a war out here and we don't need you. When you get back there you can tell them who sent you and why."

He leaned back in his chair and stared at us, letting his words sink in. I felt as though a Mousetrap had exploded in my face. A whole year of preparation and now this. He was sending me back to Washington—to a desk job, no less. All that schooling, all that "training," all those fancy restaurants, those jaunts up and down the coast, the ratrace to find lodgings, the ten thousand miles it took to get here—all for naught.

Jud, soft spoken, broke the silence. "Captain, can I speak to you in my office?" he said quietly. The two went into his office and closed the door. We heard them but couldn't understand what they were saying. Cal, still sweating, whispered, "Good. I hope he does send us back." All he wanted was to be with his new wife in Pittsburgh. I wanted the opposite. Returning to Washington was unthinkable. Having gotten this close to things I wanted to stay, come hell or high water.

The captain returned and sat down. Whatever the exec said or did had mollified him. His face wasn't as red and he spoke more calmly. "OK, you two," he said, "We won't act on this right now. You're to go out to the BOQ (Bachelor Officers' Quarters) and wait. Check in each day here until we've decided what we're going to do with you."

Finally outside, Cal was annoyed at the decision to keep us there. "Damn," he said, "for a minute I really thought we'd be going back. I just want to be with my bride. This is a life for single guys like you but I don't want to be a hero.

"Well, whatever happens I guess we can forget about Mousetraps for a while," I replied, "And wasn't that a nice chat we had with the captain?" He looked at me. We laughed in nervous relief, then headed for the BOQ.

(Note: From here on the word "mousetrap" will not be capitalized, to signify the end of the top secret mousetrap caper.)

ASW Projector Mark 5,
The Mousetrap.
National Archives Photo
RG80G No.21909

Mousetraps 49

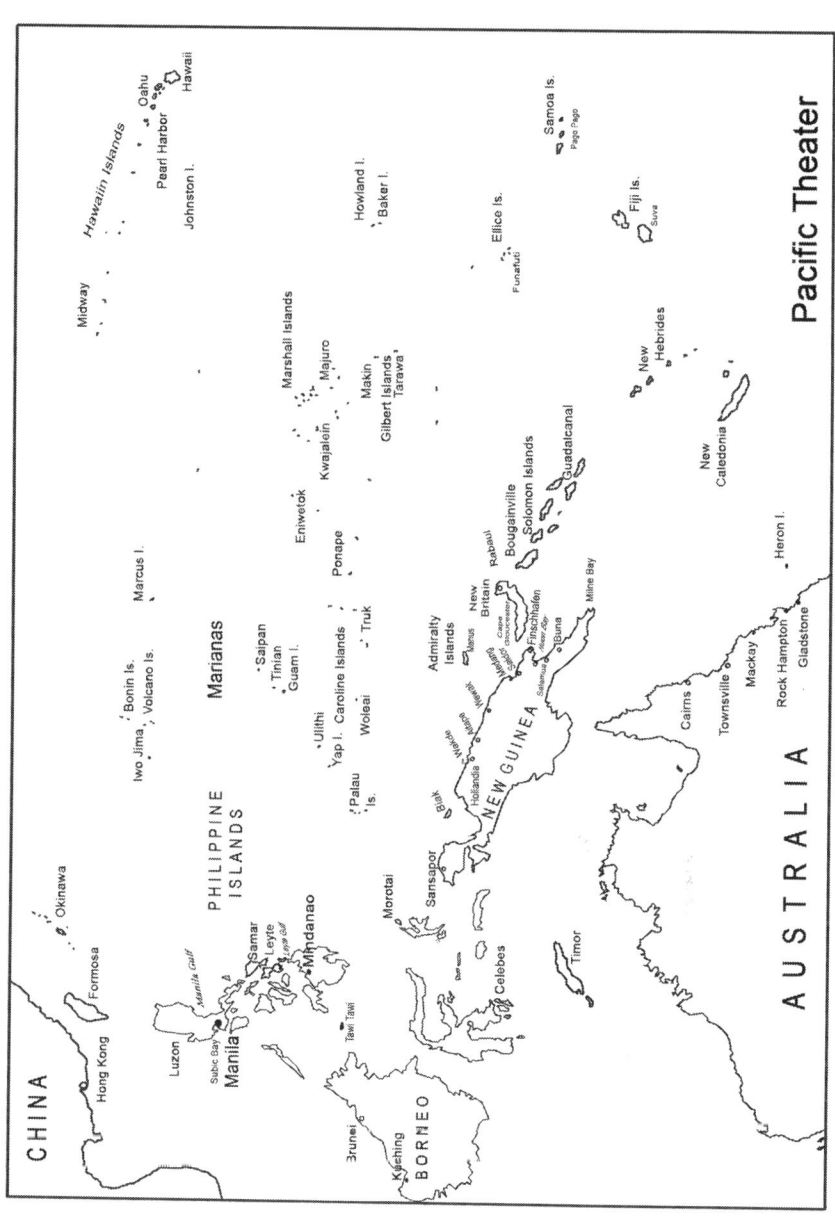

Noumea

Three days passed before Cal and I were summoned to Captain Henkle's office. This time the captain was much more relaxed. He told us they needed a Base Gunnery officer on Espiruto Santo, an island north of New Caledonia, and he was sending Miller. I was to remain in Noumea and assist the Base Gunnery Officer there. Back at the BOQ Cal packed his gear and left. We never saw each other again but whenever I see a coconut I think of Cal Miller.

> *March 16, 1943. SC 648 departs Bora Bora enroute to Pago Pago, Samoa. Starboard shaft breaks down, necessitating return to Bora Bora for underwater inspection.*
> *March 20, 1943. SC 648 returns to Pago Pago on one engine.*
> *March 30, 1943. SC 648 arrives Suva, Fiji Islands.*
> *March 31, 1943. SC 648 departs Suva in company with SC 698 enroute to Noumea, New Caledonia.*

The Base Gunnery Officer in Noumea was an Annapolis graduate, a career navy lieutenant, Lt. Brandt. He had been Damage Control Officer on the USS Chicago, a cruiser badly damaged and subsequently sunk as a result of the battle of Rennels Island. It was a harrowing experience for everyone on board and many lives were lost. Lieutenant Brandt was awarded a Silver Star for his meritorious performance during the battle. Though his physical wounds healed, Brandt was psychologically damaged. His hands shook, he ground his teeth, grimaced, and suffered from depression.

Brandt's office was in the same Quonset hut as Captain Henkle's and it was to be my office also, although there was no desk for me, just an extra chair. As Base Gunnery Officer, Brandt was responsible for arranging daily target practice sessions for navy vessels in the area. Each morning he placed calls to the Port Director and the Air Command and made the arrangements. It took less than half an hour to determine what ships would participate and for how long. Once the arrangements were made, he had nothing more to do for the rest of the day. My job was to assist him with this. He must have realized how ridiculous this was but we never discussed it because he wasn't someone you could get close to. Once the target arrangements were made he retreated into his world of sitting, staring, and occasionally writing letters, and I was on my own.

The old feelings of uselessness and frustration returned. Here I was in the middle of a war, ready and willing to make a contribution, but with no real job and no future. I felt like a misfit in a world where everyone except me was doing something useful. It didn't make sense. I decided the only way to maintain my sanity and morale was to keep busy. Remembering Captain Henkle's harangue, I signed up for a correspondence course in celestial navigation. I had to get the captain's approval for this. I figured this act of self-improvement would not only help me but would make points with him, which it did.

BOQ was an expanse of Quonset huts housing just about everyone passing through or staying in Noumea. The facilities were better than primitive, but not by much. Each hut had a galvanized roof, wooden floor, insulated walls, and ten or twelve cots, each with mosquito netting to ward off mosquitoes as big as flies. We were told not to worry about malaria because the New Caledonia eucalyptus tree was supposed to be a natural enemy of the malarial type mosquito. Even so, there were numerous cases of malaria and dengue fever. (It turns out that eucalyptus is effective in controlling the insects because it absorbs so much water that it drains swamps, leaving them no habitat for breeding. Otherwise, the idea that it would "ward off" mosquitoes was a little misguided.) The water was always lukewarm, no matter whether it was for drinking, taking showers, or washing clothes. Buckets were provided for the latter.

There was little close comradeship because men were constantly coming and going through the BOQ, many staying only a night or two while awaiting transportation to a ship based somewhere else. Anyone staying more than a week was regarded as almost a "permanent" resident. Most who came down from Guadalcanal seemed dejected and withdrawn. A writer from the Herald Tribune named Joe Driscoll came and went. A correspondent for Newsweek named Whipple was more or less "permanent." He had recently returned from Guadalcanal, where he'd been covering the campaign. He became somewhat a fixture. He would stay out half the night at one of several off-limit bars, then return in drunken hilarity, singing and telling stories and jokes before finally falling asleep. He slept past noon every day, skipping lunch to go sunbathing in the afternoon. In the evening he repeated the routine of the night before, drinking his dinner and going on his round of pubs while looking for stories.

Another BOQ "permanent" resident was an Episcopalian navy chaplain from North Carolina named Westbrook. He made himself popular by playing poker, taking a drink, and mildly cussing on rare occasions. While in San Francisco I had acquired a Varga calendar for 1943. The Varga pinup girl had been made famous by Esquire magazine; each issue had a two-page spread of her drawn by the artist Alberto Vargas, who signed himself "Varga." Once I thought I'd have some fun with Chaplain Westbrook. When he wasn't around I placed one of the Varga girl pictures on the wall over his cot. It didn't take him long to find out who did it. On the following day the Varga picture over his cot was missing and mounted over my cot was a picture of Christ with a quotation that read, "Wherefore I say to thee, her sins, many as they are, shall be forgiven her because she has loved much. But he to whom little is forgiven, loves little. Luke 7:47."

Not far from the BOQ was a large slope of ground that formed a natural amphitheater. A large screen at the bottom of the slope made it an ideal outdoor movie theater. Every night it was packed with servicemen who came to see old black-and-white movies featuring James Cagney, Sylvia Sidney, and other Hollywood stars of the time. Everyone brought a piece of corrugated cardboard or a wooden board to sit on. One innovator fashioned a chair out of an old crate, complete with padded seat and armrests. You'd always bring oilskins because it rained frequently. The rain didn't discourage anyone. You'd pull the oilskin over you and keep your eyes glued to the screen without complaining. Sometimes it rained so hard it drowned out the soundtrack. All of us huddled under wet oilskins on that sloping hill resembled a convention of tortoises. When the projector broke down, as happened frequently, the audience groaned and booed. They'd shout expletives at the operator, each more colorful than the other, until everyone was laughing in frustration.

The food wasn't very good. We ate Spam about three times a week, prepared in different ways to disguise it, but everyone knew what it was and hated it. There was little fresh milk and the eggs were powdered. The vegetables and fruits were canned, the bread made from sourdough. Pepperidge Farm makes delicious sourdough bread but the sourdough bread we ate in Noumea filled one's mouth with a bitter tingle because the dough hadn't fermented properly. We rarely had beef or chicken, but Australian mutton, with its high fat content was common and unpopular.

Many of the men who'd returned from Guadalcanal wore a gaunt, lonely look called the "thousand-yard stare."

They'd stand or sit, just staring, waiting to be told what to do next, responding listlessly to any attempt at conversation. I heard one marine say to another, "The people in the states don't realize there's a war going on." I watched another as he walked across a dusty road without looking right or left, directly in front of a jeep going by. The driver swerved and swore but the marine paid no attention, just kept walking.

With lots of extra time on my hands I got in the habit of reading the daily newspaper, La France Australe, which contained a half-page of world news printed in English. One morning I spotted a reference to Kearny, New Jersey, in an article about world soccer. Another day there was an ad offering conversational French lessons. Having nothing better to do, and having taken two years of French while in college, I answered the ad. The teacher's name was M. Philippe Le Chartier de Sedouy. During our first hourly lesson he talked nonstop in French and I understood almost nothing he said. After the third session I began to understand some of the phrases and as the lessons progressed I became a little more accustomed to it and began learning how to think in French.

The teacher talked about his life. M. Sedouy was a mining engineer who had married a Belgian countess. They came to New Caledonia in 1937, where he worked in an iron mine with connections to a Japanese company. The company dissolved with the outbreak of war. The Japanese departed, leaving him without a job. He and his wife were interned while being investigated by the U.S. for a possible connection with the Japanese, but they were released after only a few months. During her confinement his wife became infatuated with another internee, which led to their divorce. M. Sedouy was now spending his time translating a history of New Caledonia into English and teaching French while waiting to go back to France.

April 3, 1943. SC 648 arrives Noumea, New Caledonia

Noumea was a mixture of free French, Indo-Chinese, Filipinos, Kanakas, Australians, and New Zealanders. There were some Chinese and even a few questionable Japanese. Added to this was the large influx of American soldiers, sailors, and marines. The language commonly spoken by all except Americans was French. The streets were unpaved, hot, and dusty, and when it rained they turned into rutted mudflats. Many brown-skinned natives stood around, some looking quite wild and ferocious with their bushy, dyed hairdos. The native women used henna to make their hair red and the men used peroxide to make theirs blonde. Most of the men were friendly stevedores or laborers, singing and joking as they worked. They always saluted, looking at you sideways as you passed by. If you said "Hello, Harry" they'd smile and laugh, exposing their teeth, blackened by years of chewing betel nut, a narcotic. Kanakas women wore shapeless moo-moos of flimsy material in bright green, pink, blue, or yellow. Apparently, early missionaries had been offended by the natives' nakedness and convinced the women to wear the moo-moos. We used to argue about whether they were wearing underclothes beneath. It was common to see two barefooted Kanakas women squatting on their haunches chewing and chatting in their strange language. Incidentally, "Kanakas" means "human being" in Hawaiian.

Once Lt. Brandt and I drove in a jeep to a pig farm sixty miles north of Noumea to make a deal with a farmer to supply the base with fresh pork. The countryside we rode through looked very much like Pennsylvania or northwestern New Jersey with its rolling hills, though the plentiful green vegetation was of a different kind. Bamboo, banana, and eucalyptus trees were everywhere, with an occasional palm tree dotting the landscape. The owner of the pig farm, an elderly Frenchman, cordially invited us to stay for lunch. We ate pork flavored strongly with garlic, kidney beans with rice, and a dessert of fresh bananas from one of his trees. The negotiations were successful and the base had lots of fresh pork dinners after that.

There was a French souvenir shop in Noumea called the O. K. Gift Shop. It was cleaner and neater than most of the shops. Walking past it one evening, I saw a polished wooden war club in the window. It looked interesting so I went in to practice my French with the shop lady. She showed me the club and explained that natives at the extreme north end of the island, who used it in their dances and rituals, had made it. She went on about the "object d'art extraordinaire" and the "tres jolie piece."

"Mais combien cout cet object, le tresure, l'objet extraordinaire?" I asked.

"Mais oui, monsieur, le tresure offrit a quatres milles francs!" She wanted 4,000 francs for it, which was about $100. I learned the O. K. Gift Shop wasn't very OK. Their prices were too high and much of their stuff was imported, some from the United States.

In Noumea I had lots of time to write letters, choosing a variety of subjects just to keep my mind active. In one letter to my parents:

> The other day I was walking up a hill and passed a group of sailors who were walking up more slowly. I overheard one of them ask another, "Who was that French philosopher who said 'Man is his most natural self in the animal state'?" I could hardly believe my ears. How could such an erudite question come from a group of bearded, dusty, hot, tired sailors with a reputation for being interested only in women, drinking, and gambling? It only reinforces something I read recently that said the men in today's navy are of very high caliber and are very intelligent. I've gotten to know a career warrant officer in my hut who says he is amazed at the change in the navy's personnel since the war broke out. There is no comparison, he claims, the intelligence and keen-mindedness of both enlisted men and officers in the reserve is very high.

In spite of my efforts to stay busy and make the most of things I began feeling the stress of inactivity. The fighting was hundreds of miles away. My job as assistant to Lt. Brandt was ridiculous and I brooded about being so useless while there was a war going on. I was on the verge of asking Captain Henkle for transfer to a different assignment, one that would use my abilities such as they were. My relationship with the captain had improved since the day Miller and I had been on the receiving end of his tongue-lashing, probably because I had signed up for the navigation correspondence course and told him I hoped to get sea duty some day. My decision to request different duty coincided with orders the captain had just received from COMSOPAC (Commander South Pacific Forces) directing him to appoint someone as Armed Guard Unit Inspector. That someone, the captain said, was going to be me. I was to inspect Armed Guard units on all the merchant ships passing through the port of Noumea.

The Armed Guard was an extension of the navy's defense against enemy submarines and aircraft. All merchant vessels were equipped with guns for use when attacked, whether alone or in convoy, plus staffed with navy personnel, including an officer. Arming merchant ships proved to be an excellent means of defense. During the war Armed Guard units had several engagements with the enemy, performing with valor. It was important for the units to be well trained and prepared for attack at all times and it made sense to have a measure of control, with periodic inspections.

As inspector, I was assigned a jeep and had the use of both the motor and the boat pool. Whenever a merchant ship arrived in Noumea I would send a message notifying it that an inspection of their unit would be made at a certain time on the following day. After the first few inspections I became familiar with the job, and life settled into a routine. I'd have a boat take me out to the ship to be inspected and would be met by the navy officer in charge of the

Armed Guard unit. Often the officers outranked me but because they were under inspection they were careful to be very respectful. In each case they'd have their crew lined up in dress uniforms and standing at attention while we passed by, inspecting. We'd then look over their quarters, making sure their bunks were neatly made, shoes shined, and all that. We'd inspect the ordnance and if anything was amiss the officer would explain. Armed Guard units received excellent training before shipping out and I seldom found anything wrong. During one of these inspections I heard my name called and turned around to see a smiling John Parker, good friend of Dan Hodges, Steve's younger brother. John was on his first cruise as a merchant marine cadet in training to be an officer. He sported a beard and was in greasy coveralls from working on one of the lifeboat motors. Later we got together and caught up on home news.

I suppose I should have been satisfied with the inspector's job but I wasn't happy about the prospect of serving out the war as an Armed Guard inspector or as a land-based officer. I longed to be on one of the many ships that came and went, headed for some secret and significant rendezvous with destiny (or so I fantasized). My longing to be part of the seagoing navy became obsessive. I decided to ask Captain Henkle for a transfer to sea duty.

One day after making an Armed Guard inspection, I returned to the base in the early afternoon fully primed to request an audience with Captain Henkle. In my mind I had carefully rehearsed what I would say. My purpose was to be listed for transfer to the first available duty on board a ship—any ship, it didn't matter as long as it was a U.S. navy ship. All keyed up, I went to his office only to be told by the yeoman that the captain had been summoned to Admiral Halsey's office for an important meeting. As I stood there, feeling very let down, another officer paused to chat. Ensign Stan Wawroski was a bomb disposal officer who also worked in Captain Henkle's offices and with whom I had become friendly.

"What's up, Ted? You look unhappy," Stan said.

I had already talked to Stan previously about wanting to get on a ship. I told him about how I'd primed myself to talk to Henkle only to find him away from the office.

"Hey, y'know what?" he said, "There's a guy on a subchaser that just got in a few days ago. He's a friend of mine from basic training. He doesn't like the duty and from the way he talks he'd give his right arm to get off."

"Boy, I'd like to meet him."

"Well, I'm meeting him later for a beer. Why don't you come along?"

"Sure thing," I said, perking up.

Later that afternoon Stan and I went over to the bar at the Noumea Officers' Club. The bar set some kind of record for being the longest bar in the South Pacific. A couple of officers were at one end and Stan's friend was at the other. He was Richard E. "Dick" Vernor, and after Stan introduced us Dick and I were soon engaged in conversation about our respective jobs.

"So, you're off a ship?" I asked.

He laughed. "Well, if you could call what I'm on a ship I guess you could say I'm off a ship, but as far as I'm concerned it's a pretty sorry excuse for a ship. But to answer your question, yes, I'm off a ship. I wish I was off it for good." He raised his glass and took a swallow.

"Stan said it's a subchaser."

"Yep, it's a subchaser."

"One of those hundred and ten footers?"

"That's right."

"Has it got mousetraps?"

"Yes, why?"

"I'm supposed to be an expert on mousetraps," I said, and gave him some background about my mousetrap trainng, including the story of the sweaty meeting Cal and I had in Capt. Henkle's office.

"What's the matter with the ship?"

"Almost everything's the matter with it," he said, shaking his head. "I hate it. I can't stand the skipper. He almost sank it on the way across. Yes, I mean it. He almost sank it. He almost blew it out of the water."

"Almost blew it out of the water?"

"We were on our way out here and we had a sub contact. He had everybody at general quarters and he started making a run and, mind you, this was going to be with live depth charges. For some reason he had set the speed at only 7 knots. That was his attack speed. We were standing together on the flying bridge. I said to him, 'Captain, it's too slow, the charges are set for only fifty feet,' and he said, 'Don't tell me how to run this ship,' or words to that effect. Well, the first charge went off at fifty feet and almost blew us out of the water. I was never so scared in my life. It bent the port shaft so badly we couldn't use it. We had only one screw the rest of the trip."

"Has it been repaired?"

"No, we're waiting to get into drydock here."

"Forgetting about that incident, what kind of skipper is he?"

"In my humble opinion, the guy's an egotistical, Texas blowhard and you can't tell him anything. But it isn't only that. The ship's too cramped, too rough, and too dirty. It's not like a navy ship should be. They call it a subchaser but it wouldn't be able to fight its way out of a paper bag. If we ever came face to face with a submarine we'd be a sitting duck. We'd be dead."

Dick was the Third Officer. I asked him about the Exec.

"He's ticked too."

"About what?"

"Same things—the skipper, the lousy, cramped conditions. He's newly married and misses his wife."

"How about the crew?"

He shrugged. "The crew's ok, but the whole ship's a mess. It's not just the captain. Everything's damp or wet, there's no room, no privacy. It's so cramped everyone's crawling over each other. At sea it's rough. You get sick. The food's pretty bad. We have to beg food from other ships. There's cockroaches. There's no laundry. You can't take a shower."

"No shower at all?"

"Only when we get into port. Not when we're at sea."

"Are you supposed to be operating out of Noumea?"

"For the time being, but there's talk of sending us to Australia. We've been here almost three weeks. We're waiting to get that shaft fixed. We've done a couple of harbor patrols, but mostly we've lain around. If I could get off or get a transfer, I'd do it in a minute."

Stan excused himself and left. I ordered another beer.

"This one's on me," I said. "Y'know, listening to you I'm thinking maybe you'd be happier in a job like mine."

"Tell me about it," he said.

"Well, it's pretty easy, actually. The inspections themselves are no problem and I get plenty of time in between so I'm on my own a lot. And there's a couple of real perks. I've got a jeep and the boat pool's at my disposal so I can go anywhere on the island or in the harbor as I please."

"Why are you telling me this? It sounds like a perfect setup. Are they looking for another inspector?"

"No, but as you were talking, I was thinking, uh, well, I've been wanting to get some sea duty, and maybe you and I could consider switching jobs."

We studied each other for a moment. I could tell he was thinking, "Why would anyone want to chuck a job like that after what I've told him about the subchaser?" The dreamer versus the practical was churning inside me. Matter-of-fact about most things, I fantasized about some things. Fantasy was winning. The opportunity to get on a ship was irresistible. I had watched too many movies, seen too many ships coming and going. Like being in love with the wrong girl, my head said "no" but my heart longed to be on a ship. I rationalized. Maybe he's exaggerating about things; maybe the ship's not all that bad; there's two sides to every story.

"I heard a couple of guys out here traded jobs," I said, "They arranged it right here. They didn't have to go through BuPers or anything. I think they only had to get an approval from each of their C.O.s."

He said, "Yes, I think that's right. I heard something like that also."

"Y'know, maybe it isn't as bad as you say," I said. "I know it's not easy but I'd be willing to take a shot at being third officer. That is, I've been wanting to get on a ship and—"

"Are you serious?"

"Absolutely."

"What about your CO?"

"I think he'll OK it. He knows I want sea duty. What about your skipper, the Texas bragger?"

"Oh, that's no problem. He'd be glad to see me go. He and I just don't see eye to eye. Are you sure you're willing to go for this? You haven't even seen the ship."

"Yeah, I know. By the way, what's its number, and what's your skipper's name?"

"It's the SC 648 and his name is Spaugh," he replied. "Paul Allen Spaugh. He never lets you forget he's from Texas."

"He may not want me any more than he wants you, and the same goes for Capt. Henkle about you." I said.

We were each thinking this was too good to be true. We ordered a final beer to toast our futures and figure how to put the plan into effect.

"You'll like the job," I said, "You're pretty much your own boss and you can get around."

He smiled. "Wish I could say the same for what you're getting into. I'll say this frankly, I can't see how anyone would want to give up what you've got after what I've told you, but I guess it's every man for himself in this war."

The next day was spent closing the deal. I went out to the subchaser, met Paul Allen Spaugh, answered a few questions, and got his OK, then Dick Vernor and I came into the base and got Captain Henkle to approve his part of the transfer. The captain had mellowed considerably since the first day Cal and I appeared in his office. Still somewhat gruff, he nevertheless approved of this latest change. When he handed me my orders, he stood up and shook my hand and wished me luck. Dick and I then went over to Admiral "Bull" Halsey's office to finish the paperwork. An hour later we each had our orders.

Third Officer

On special occasions in the traditional navy, whenever a V.I.P. boards a warship the crew "pipes the side," which means everyone is in full dress, standing at attention, while a boatswain's whistle is "piped" and eight or ten sailors called "side boys" form a lane on the quarterdeck through which he passes. Sometimes there's a band and a welcoming speech.

My first boarding on SC 648 was less formal, to say the least. She was docked in a nest that included two other subchasers and a couple of YMS minesweepers. When I arrived no one seemed to be aboard except a shirtless enlisted man in dirty denim cutoffs who grabbed my duffel bag while I stepped aboard. The 648's log entry for April 24, 1943, reads:

> 0902. Ens. Theodore R. Treadwell O-V(S) USNR reported on board for duty. No further remarks. Gerald M. Lively, Executive Officer. Paul A. Spaugh, Lt.(jg) USNR Commanding.

The lack of ceremony didn't matter. In my starry-eyed view this grungy assortment of wood and steel was my ship at last—the slickest, meanest, fightingest warship in the whole damn navy, the most gorgeous ship that ever sailed the seven seas!

The enlisted man led me into the pilothouse to an open hatch next to the helm. A ladder in the hatch led to the radio shack below. As I climbed down, my head struck the sill of the hatch with a good thwack. Paul Allen Spaugh, C.O., stood at the foot of the ladder. "Ouch," he said for me. "You'll get used to that. Come on in." He led me into the wardroom, where Jerry Lively, the Exec, was standing. The room was small and cramped, with a double bunk against the port bulkhead and a single bunk against the starboard bulkhead. Two folding-top desks and a file cabinet stood against the aft bulkhead while along the forward bulkhead was a coffee stand and a small bookcase with a Tommy gun and a rifle mounted on the bulkhead over them. A narrow door on the starboard side of the bulkhead, near the captain's bunk, led to a small head with a tiny basin, toilet, and cramped shower stall. An overhead vent connected to a gooseneck topside furnished fresh air. The air was circulated by oscillating fans mounted near the overhead in each corner of the room. Incidentally, these fans never stopped during the twenty-three months I was aboard, nor, so far as I know, did they ever get oiled.

Lt. (jg) Paul Allen Spaugh stood over six feet tall, with arms and shoulders rippling with the muscles of a swimmer, tapering down to a 32" waist. His blue eyes and deeply bronzed complexion were that of a modern-day Leif Ericson. He smiled a lot and spoke with a Texas accent. Born and raised in Galveston, he had been captain of the Texas A&M swim team. As a teenager he had considerable small craft experience, an advantage that led to his being placed in the Captains-in-Training group at SCTC. He had taken command shortly before the ship left Miami for the Pacific.

Lt. (jg) Gerald M. Lively, executive officer, was shorter, with a slightly stocky build. His face was round and waxy, a thin mustache on his upper lip. He spoke in a soft voice and didn't smile much. He had earned a law degree at St. Louis University, married his high school sweetheart, and no sooner set up practice in Kansas City than the war broke out. He joined the navy to avoid being drafted. He saw no romance or adventure in being on a subchaser. He wanted only to get done with the war and return to his bride, Selma. He was a sharp contrast to Captain Spaugh. We sat on canvas folding chairs and Spaugh did most of the talking. He spoke highly of the crew.

"You'll learn the ropes in no time with guys like these," he said. "The chief motor mac knows more about our diesels than anyone in the whole navy. I never saw a guy who could do so much with so little. We get no spare parts but he keeps us going and I don't know how he does it.

"We've got an electrician's mate who used to work on railroads repairing their signal systems. He knows more about the circuitry on this ship than the guys who built it. We have a quartermaster who could take over the ship tomorrow if I let him. The yeoman, I couldn't get along without him." He turned his head and called, "Beck, come in and meet our new third officer." Beck, the yeoman, whose desk was just outside the wardroom, entered. He was clean-cut, intelligent-looking, with a broad smile. "Welcome aboard, sir," he said, shaking hands, "I hope you won't be sorry. It's not the most comfortable life in the world."

"Go on, Beck, you never had it so easy," Spaugh said.

"Yeah, just like home, Cap'n," Beck replied, smiling. He went back to his desk.

Spaugh said, "I'd be lost without him. All these guys are phenomenal. They make my job easy and they'll do the same for you. Right, Jerry?"

"Right. And don't forget Swett," Jerry replied.

"Yeah, that's right," Spaugh said. "We have a guy, his name is Swett, a real character. I swear, he can fix anything. Anything. I never knew anyone who could figure things out like Swett. The guy's always coming up with crazy ideas that work."

The remainder of the day was spent mostly with Jerry. We took a tour of the ship and I kept bumping my head and elbows on things. Everything was cramped. I met most of the crewmembers. One of the responsibilities of the third officer was communications. I spent a long time with Jerry and Beck looking at and sorting manuals, codebooks, and various confidential papers.

I thought to myself, this is the best day of my navy career. The months of frustration are finally over. Now I'm a member of a ship's company on a real navy warship! I'll make the most of every minute, every hour, every day. She was my ship and I would become a part of her. She was the most beautiful ship in the South Pacific!

During my first week we were either anchored or in dry dock, giving me a good opportunity to familiarize myself with the ship and get acquainted with the crew. Jerry was a good mentor. Years later in a news interview about his navy years Jerry referred to me as "a gung-ho eager-beaver type." Maybe so, but my recollection is one of complete ignorance and incompetence that somehow had to be overcome. Actually, after only a week I was beginning to feel at home.

We laid at anchor for three days and then went into dry dock for repairs to the starboard shaft and screw that had been damaged during the depth charge attack that Ensign Vernor had told me about in the Officers' Club. The dry dock was a navy ARD2, a giant floating repair dock that could hold three subchasers end to end. Heavy steel doors on each end opened and closed to permit ships to enter as in a canal lock. Ours was the first ship to enter, followed by YMS 97, a minesweeper. The doors closed and pumps removed water, a process that took more than two hours. As the water level inside the caisson went down workers adjusted the shipways so the two vessels would stay properly supported. The crews remained on board. The walls of the caisson rose high above us.

I was standing at the rail with Jerry, watching the activity, when I heard someone calling my name. High above on the caisson, Steve Hodges was waving down at us. With the 648 secured, I scrambled up the ladder for a great back-slapping reunion. The last time we had seen each other was in Boston at the B-School the day of the Pearl Harbor attack. He'd just come down to Noumea from Guadalcanal, where he flew Kingfisher scout planes for observation and harbor patrol. The flyers on Guadalcanal lived in tents and foxholes under steady bombing attacks. Steve had contracted malaria and was stopping in Noumea on his way to Sydney for a week's R & R, then back to the States for recovery. He had been taking heavy doses of atabrine—the standard treatment for malaria in those days—that had turned his skin yellow. He'd lost thirty pounds while in Guadalcanal and looked pretty thin. His spirits were fine. I kidded him about looking so skinny. He said, "Yeah, I got so thin the guys called me the 'Assless Wonder'." We had an hour or so to catch up on news before he left for Sydney. He gave me a ring made from a U.S. half-dollar, with a gold tooth mounted on it. He said a marine got the tooth off a dead Jap and mounted it on a ring he made. I still have it somewhere.

There wasn't much time and Steve had to leave. I thought, "He's done with the war and now he's going home," figuring his days in uniform were over. Little did I realize the navy's need for officers, particularly experienced officers. He returned to the States for several months then came back out on a carrier where he saw plenty more action.

After a day in dry dock we had a new shaft and propeller and were floated out. We refueled, replenished our fresh water and food, and then prepared for departure to Australia. On the afternoon of May 5 we rendezvoused with four other subchasers bound for Brisbane, Australia. SC 731 was SOPA (Senior Officer Present Afloat) and SCs 981, 698, 732, and 648 made up the balance of the little fleet. We'd been assigned to the Seventh Service Force, part of the newly formed Seventh Fleet under Rear Admiral Daniel E. Barbey. Seventh Fleet was soon to be nicknamed "MacArthur's Navy" because Admiral Barbey took his orders directly from General MacArthur, the commander of Southwest Pacific Forces. General MacArthur's headquarters were in Brisbane.

Jerry took the 8:00 to midnight watch and I had the midwatch, from midnight to 4:00. The captain would have the morning watch, from 4:00 to 8:00. As the ship's navigator, he could get star sights at daybreak. The watches were set at Condition 3, which meant standing watch for four hours with eight hours off. Condition 2 would have meant four-on-four-off but the war had moved further north and the waters between Noumea and Australia were considered relatively free of enemy ships and subs. The voyage would take three days and would be my first experience as a watch officer underway.

Once out of the harbor the five subchasers took positions in a simple V formation with SC 731 leading. Our ship was trim and neat (at least in my eyes) as it headed west toward the open sea. Several of us stood on the flying bridge making conversation, enjoying the breeze and watching the blazing Pacific sunset. I was thinking: This is the life, by George; how could such beauty ever be matched? If only we were cruising out here for the fun of it! I've been on this ship a week and already I feel like a salty old mariner! High adventure is out there over the horizon! What a lucky guy am I! At last I've got a job in this war and I've got my sea duty! This is it! To be on a United States navy warship is what it's all about! Still fantasizing, I went below to get some sleep before going on watch. The breeze had stiffened, causing us to pitch and roll a bit but I felt no signs of seasickness and this made me feel pretty good. Stripping to my skivvies and climbing into my bunk, I thought, "Guess I've arrived in this man's navy."

I'd no sooner lain down, however, when the ship began pitching, pounding, and rolling with increasing force. The hull smacked down, making a loud banging noise. I thought: Were we in a storm? What's causing all this banging around and motion? Were we in trouble? The ship was twisting with each pitch, causing my body to rock from one side of the berth to the other. Now I realized why there were sideboards on the bunks. We seemed to be hitting some real heavy weather. The ship was careening with tremendous force, first in an upward, rolling motion, then plunging violently down, thudding as it hit the water, trembling, then up again, rolling, hesitating and crashing down, no two cycles exactly the same except they were all bad. The wooden ship creaked and groaned with every movement. I wanted to get up and see for myself but was afraid I'd be seasick if I stood up. Spaugh had come down and was lying in his bunk. Looking across at him, I could see that he was sleeping like a baby. Good Lord, why wasn't he up and about in weather like this? What kind of ship's captain could be so irresponsible? How could anyone sleep on this roller coaster?

I must have dozed off. Someone was tapping my shoulder.

"Time for the watch, sir." It was the quartermaster, Hulse.

The ship was pitching and rolling unmercifully.

"Uh, oh, OK. Everything OK topside?" I asked.

"Yes sir, everything's fine" he said, "The wind has freshened up but the skies are clear and everything's fine. Does it feel rough to you, sir?"

"Uh, well, I guess I've got to learn how this ship behaves," I muttered, trying to put on a good front although I knew he knew better. His reply about conditions had been reassuring but my stomach wasn't convinced. Hulse left to return topside.

I had to get up and dress, and I felt seasick. I eased myself to the deck, which was rolling and pitching wildly. On the opposite side of the wardroom Spaugh was in his captain's bunk sound asleep. My legs were like rubber. Everything in the room was moving. Nausea gripped me. I had just enough time to stagger to the head. The seasickness was immediate and powerful. Everything spewed out in a violent tube of projectile vomit, splattering the sides and top of the porcelain toilet. Bending over it my knees wobbled. The nausea was all-consuming. Swaying, I heaved until there was nothing left but dry spittle, then heaved again, with violent cramping that hurt my stomach muscles. It was ten minutes before I had to be on the bridge. Dry heaving, I wiped the toilet clean and came out of the head. Spaugh was still sleeping soundly. I dressed awkwardly, dry mouthed, tasting, smelling, and feeling like vomit. "So this is the life, eh?" I thought.

I dragged myself to the ladder past the radio shack with Esser, RM/3c, on duty and climbed up into the pilot house. At the top of the ladder Jerry was sitting in the tall chair known as the "Captain's Chair." Touhy, BM/2c, was at the helm and Beebe, QM/3c, stood in the background. These men, including Moyer the sonarman and Esser below, were experienced men. I was thankful for that because it would make the watch much easier. The blackness of night thankfully concealed my wretchedness.

Jerry said, "How do you feel? You want some coffee?"

"I'm fine," I lied. "No coffee, thanks," tightening my stomach muscles to conceal the retching. "What's happening?"

"Nothing much. Pretty routine. C'mon. I'll show you where the other ships are." He went outside to the quarterdeck while I followed, grabbing things to steady my rubbery legs. The ship was pitching and rolling (badly, I thought) but no one on watch seemed to be minding it so I had to assume (correctly) that things were normal.

"Yo, Swett! You awake?" Jerry hollered in the direction of the crow's nest.

"You just woke me up," Swett sang out. "Nice ride up here. Wanna try it?"

Jerry smiled. "Not now thanks. Some other time."

The crow's nest swayed crazily with every motion of the ship. Salt spume splattered against its canvas sheath and Swett ducked.

"How can he stand it up there?" I asked.

"It's a rough ride," Jerry said. "That's why we change that station every two hours. It's the worst watch station on the ship. George Green will relieve him at 2:00. Swett there is one of our best men."

In the fresh air my head cleared and my stomach relaxed somewhat. The ship bounced and rolled along, the salt spray occasionally hitting our faces. Jerry pointed out the other subchasers. We were cruising at 12 knots in box formation, keeping station 800 yards apart in each direction. We were on the starboard quarter of the box, following SC 981 dead ahead, with SC 698 broad on our port beam. SC 731, SOPA, was in the corner diagonally across the box from us.

"You can see them pretty well," Jerry said. "Just maintain this position. Touhy's good on the helm and he'll stay on course OK. We're on 254 degrees True. He keeps his eye on the ship ahead and we're supposed to stay on 254 for the next several hours. One thing you'll have to watch. Make sure he follows the 981, not our 40 mm gun.

"What do you mean?"

"Sometimes at night when you're following another ship, the way the gun is mounted forward, the muzzle sticks up in front of you just enough to confuse it for a ship. If you or the helmsman get tired or you're not paying attention you could fall for it. Touhy's pretty good and it probably won't happen, but you should know about it. C'mon, let's take a look at the chart."

Back in the little compartment aft of the helm that we called the chart room we leaned over the dimly lighted chart with its penciled track headed directly for Australia.

"You can plot it as we go along, or you can have Beebe do it. You don't have to worry about Beebe. He's dependable. And he'll keep track of other details, including calling out the relief watches. You shouldn't have any trouble. If a strange ship or a light or something unusual occurs and you can't figure out what's happening, don't be afraid to wake the captain. The SOPA will probably signal you by light or by radio and clear things up but you'll have to use your own judgment. Got any questions?"

"Can't think of any, so what do I say, 'Ready to relieve the watch, sir'?"

"Good enough for me. You won't have any problems. OK, you've got it." He went below. Except for the emptiness of my stomach and an occasional retch I managed to subdue the seasick feeling and began adjusting myself to the ship's motion. It's called "getting your sea legs." I knew the men on watch wondered how this new officer would be. Anything I said would be earmarked, noted, remembered, and interpreted in their eyes as my persona. I decided to say as little as necessary and simply get to know them (and myself as officer of the deck).

Things went smoothly. We made no course or speed changes, we maintained our position well, and the experience of the men made it easy. The watch went by fairly quickly. At 4:00 I turned it over to the captain without incident, feeling like a schoolboy who's just passed an important test.

For two days we continued in the same formation, changing watches and carrying on ship routines without incident. I didn't eat until the day we made landfall, when I had a light breakfast and was able to keep it down. At 5:30 a.m. on May 8 we sighted the light on Cape Moreton and an hour later saw land on the starboard bow. By 10:00 a.m. we were cruising across Moreton Bay toward the mouth of the Brisbane River. Steaming upriver, we all crowded the rail to get our first sight of Australia. Everyone was anticipating new sights, shore liberty, and some R & R. By 4:00 p.m. we were nested with the other subchasers alongside a wharf in Brisbane.

SC 648, the author's "Ship of Dreams"

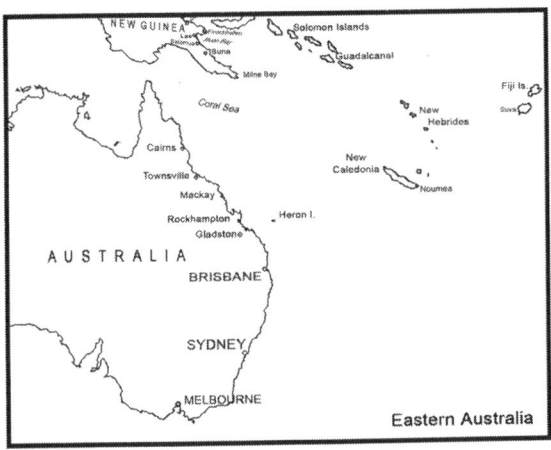

From May to August 1943 we operated along the Australian coast.

The 648 smacks into heavy seas. Note mousetraps secured to deck

Seconds later everything's awash

Australia

The first day in Brisbane was spent stocking up on food, fuel, and water. Spaugh went ashore to report and to pick up orders. The following day I had a few hours of liberty and went ashore with Hank Reentz, third officer from SC 699. The weather was cool enough to wear our dress blues. My blues had been stuffed in the duffel bag so long they were badly wrinkled and more than a little moldy so I had to work a bit to make them look good enough to wear.

In 1943 Brisbane was a bustling city of half a million people or so. The docks and wharves were cluttered with warehouses and old brick buildings. The general architecture seemed old fashioned, turn-of-the-century. It was Sunday, a bright, beautiful day, and we heard birds singing. People strolled around, many in uniform. We walked along Queen Street, Brisbane's main thoroughfare, past lots of brownstone buildings. A trolley track ran along the center of Queen Street, reminding me of Broad Street in Newark, New Jersey. We walked past a modern-looking hotel, the Lennon, where (we didn't realize it at the time) General MacArthur lived with his wife and young son.

Going by a Presbyterian church, we noticed people entering so we decided to join them. As we passed through the doorway an attractive girl stopped us and pinned a white flower on our lapels in honor of Mothers' Day. It was nice until she smiled, displaying two ugly gaps where her teeth should have been. The minister acknowledged our presence from the pulpit with an announcement about "our two American guests." An all-women choir sang familiar hymns and two babies were baptized, evoking memories that made me feel momentarily homesick.

After the service we looked for a place to eat. A restaurant with fresh fruit in the window looked pretty good so we went in and ate a great steak dinner with giant beakers of fresh cold milk followed by a dessert of fresh fruit and a big bowl of ice cream. Outside again, we climbed aboard a trolley car without the slightest idea of where it was going. Soon we were in a suburban area where a crowd was gathered at a playing field. We got off the trolley and watched a game of cricket for almost an hour, understanding very little of it. It was a day of nostalgia and memories that seemed quite distant and long ago.

Two days later SC 648 was assigned to Guard Ship duty, a formality remembered primarily for its title. One subchaser was made responsible for security at the wharf, permitting the other ships to grant liberties to more of their crew while in port. The duty rotated from one SC to another every twenty-four hours. After we were relieved of Guard Ship duty we began giving liberties to most of the crew. True to form, after one of these liberties Touhy, our boatswain's mate, ended up in sick bay as a result of head wounds sustained, he said, from "a fall down the steps of a church."

Bill Touhy was in his mid-30s, one of two older men on the ship. He was a career man in his fifteenth year in the navy, an exception to the rule that subchasers were manned mostly by young reservists. Born and raised in South Boston, he had the typical dialect of a "Southie." Husky, grizzled, and with tattoos over most of his upper body, he was 100 percent Boston Irish, full of charm one minute, shouting profanities the next. His rating of 2nd class was lower than it should have been for a man with that many years of service and was the result of too many drunken liberties, brawls, and AWOLs. He could easily have made a chief petty officer but for his weakness for the bottle. He was an excellent helmsman and liked working the helm. One night while I was on watch with him at the helm we got to talking and I mentioned that I had lived for a while in the Boston area and also that my mother had been born in Dorchester. Touhy warmed to that; he probably felt he had an ally on board—even if he was an officer. During long watches together he never tired of talking about Boston. He'd boast about having been in every precinct jail in the city and about barroom brawls that usually featured him as the victor. He described them so colorfully you could practically hear the crash of swinging doors and see the smashing of beer mugs against taproom mirrors.

He had his sentimental moments too. In a surprisingly smooth, soothing voice that held key nicely, he'd sing ditties and ballads that I'd never heard before. One of them was about three Jews talking over where they'd like to go when they died—something like "Jerusalem was good enough for Kavinsky and the Bronx OK for Cohen, but Ginsberg would take nothing but a little spot where the River Shannon flows, a shamrock on his nose"—or words to that effect. His wife was his "old lady" and she often flavored his ramblings: "When I was back in Boston I told me old lady that I'd give me right arm to be out here gettin' a crack at the Japs and now that I'm here I'd give me left arm to be back with her watchin' a hockey game. Yessir, the old lady 'n' me cuss a lot and sometimes don't speak to each other fer a week but there ain't no one like me old lady and I'd like to be with her right now. I ain't never goin' to sea again no more when I get back this time, no-siree. Not unless me old lady drives me to it.

Touhy was a poor example for some of the other crew members. Once he and Ray Bane, gunner's mate, went on liberty together. They went AWOL, not returning to the ship until the next morning. They'd gotten in a fight and both of them were badly beaten around the head. Bane's nose was still bleeding and he had a nasty head wound. Somewhat out of control, he grabbed a .45 pistol and shot it off harmlessly, startling everyone. He was quickly subdued, all the while shaking his head, saying, "I didn't mean nothin', I didn't mean nothin', Cap'n." Both Touhy and Bane were placed on report and given a captain's mast with subsequent loss of a couple of liberties. Not long after that Bane was transferred to another ship. Incidentally, Bane is one of the few crew members still living today. (Appendix D).

Brisbane at this time was the home port for lots of U.S. submarines that went on long, dangerous patrols up into enemy waters and did major damage to all kinds of Japanese shipping. We frequently escorted the subs in and out of Moreton Bay and I recall rendezvousing with SS 228 (USS Drum) when she arrived back from her fifth long dangerous cruise in Japanese waters. Those guys in the submarine service were very special. Though we didn't realize it at the time, they were the ones who were inflicting the most damage to the Japanese navy.

I was rapidly getting familiar with the ship and the routines and beginning to feel more comfortable as third officer. Jerry was a good mentor and instructor and Spaugh was a good navigator and ship handler. Watch-standing, piloting, taking pelorus bearings, learning about communication and code books—they were all becoming routine. In port I was responsible for procuring food and supplies, retrieving mail, and going on other miscellaneous errands having to do with ship's business. The small work parties on these forays gave me a chance to know some of the men. They were always trying to better their living conditions. Whether by scrounging, bargaining, swapping, or "moonlight requisition," it didn't matter as long as it contributed to the general welfare aboard ship. Getting the right food was important and, luckily, fresh food was plentiful in Brisbane. We could get fresh eggs, milk, vegetables, potatoes, ice cream, and meat. The only complaint was not enough beef and an oversupply of Australian mutton, which many of the men disliked.

It was around this time that Jerry and I had a long, unforgettable, disturbing conversation. Spaugh had gone ashore to tend to ship's business and the two of us were in the wardroom at our desks writing letters. Jerry put his pen down, leaned back. and said, "Well, how do you like it on board this ship? You feel like you're getting used to life as a sailor?"

"I like it. It beats shore duty by a mile," I replied. "I think I've even gotten over my seasickness."

He smiled. "Wait till you hit some really rough weather." He hesitated, then said, "There's something I'd like to talk to you about."

He cleared his throat. He seemed very serious. "I was wondering what you think about Spaugh."

"What I think? Uh, I don't know, why do you ask?"

"I mean, have you figured him out? Have you formed any opinions about him yet?" He was looking at me intently.

"He's fine as far as I know. He's good at handling the ship, and the men seem to respect him. I don't really know him yet; he's all Texas, I mean, he talks like a Texan and he's kind of loud. He's got a big ego. But we're all the way we are, aren't we? Why do you ask? What are you getting at? Don't you think he's a pretty good commanding officer?"

He was looking at me with a wry smile. He slowly shook his head.

"You don't really know him yet,"

"What do you mean? Am I missing something here?"

He leaned forward, elbows on his knees.

"Something happened in Miami a few days before we left to come out here. I'll tell you, but just keep quiet about it, OK? Along with some other things it's been bugging the devil out of me."

"Sure, Jerry, you've got my word."

"Have you noticed the watch he's wearing?" he asked.

"His watch? No, not really, just that he wears one."

"It doesn't belong to him. He stole it."

"He stole it? What do you mean, 'he stole it?'"

"Just what I'm saying. Listen. Here's what happened. Spaugh took command of the ship on the day Dick Vernor reported aboard. It was in the middle of January. Dick Joy had been waiting for Vernor to arrive because he could now be relieved off the ship and transferred to a DE as exec. Incidentally, he was a damn good officer and a great skipper. Everyone respected him. Well, Spaugh relieved Joy and became the new skipper and I was now the executive officer.

"We went to Miami to replace the forward gun and get mousetraps installed, plus some other repairs. It took a couple of weeks. Then we went to Key West and made a few trips back and forth to Galveston, mostly escort duty. Then we got orders to return to Miami. Well, you know how the mail gets fouled up when you're moving around so much, so we went quite a while without any mail. A few days after we got back to Miami the mail finally caught up with us and we got a big bunch—there must have been five or six sacks of mail. Spaugh likes to open the mail and distribute it, so this day he did just that. The whole crew stood around, each waiting for his name to be called. He gave out the first-class mail first, then the magazines and newspapers, and finally the packages.

"He'd given out most of the packages when he came upon a little one addressed to Lt.(jg)Richard P. Joy. I was standing alongside him. I noticed it was from Abercrombie & Fitch, you know, the high-class outfitters in New York. He held it up for everyone to see, shook it a little, and said 'Hmmm, this looks interesting, wonder what it is.' Right in front of everyone he tore the wrapper off and pulled out a leather case with Abercrombie & Fitch printed in gold on it. He opened the case and there was this beautiful chronograph wristwatch. I remembered Joy saying something about getting his watch repaired when we were in New York. It was a beauty, all right. Joy had money and it was an expensive watch.

"Well, Spaugh took the watch out of the box and strapped it on his wrist. He held it up for everyone to see and said 'Looks pretty good, huh?' He left it on his wrist and finished giving out the rest of the packages and everyone scattered to read their mail. He kept it on his wrist as though it belonged to him. When we got below I said to him, 'You're going to send that watch back, aren't you?' and he said, 'Yeah, maybe, I don't know, we'll see.'

"Well, he's been wearing that watch ever since. He's wearing it right now." Jerry's voice was very soft and low. "He has no intention of sending it back. He's a thief, Ted. He's nothing but a common thief."

I stared at him. "Maybe he intends to return it. Maybe he has every intention to send it back," I offered.

He shook his head.

"No way," he said. "You don't know him. There's other things."

"Other things? What do you mean?"

"There's been stuff missing. Little things. One of the guys—Lou George—had a nice pocketknife. He left it on the forward gun locker when he went below. He was gone for only a few minutes. When he got back it was gone. Spaugh had been with him while he was cleaning the 40 mm. No one else was around. Lou George told me about it a couple of days later. He said he asked the captain if he had seen it and Spaugh said no. George didn't say so but I could tell he didn't believe him. There's no doubt in my mind Spaugh took it. I just know he took it. But of course I can't prove it and that's what really bugs me.

I was about to say something. "Wait," he said. "There's more."

"More?"

"There's been a couple of times guys have reported money missing from their lockers. When it happened the second time we had a locker search. Of course we didn't search the wardroom."

"You mean since Spaugh's been skipper?"

"Yes. We never had anything like this before that."

"I've noticed him playing cards for money with the men," I said.

"He does worse than that. He does something no captain of a ship—or an officer—should ever do. He gets down on his hands and knees and shoots craps with the men just as though he was one of them. And the stakes aren't peanuts. They're pretty high, especially right after they've been paid."

"You mean ...?"

"Wait, let me finish. I told you about money missing. The guys who reported money missing were guys who cleaned up in the crap games—Hagmann and Newman. Like they were targeted."

I could only stare at him.

"Ted, this guy has really got me down. Everything is circumstantial. Nothing can be proved. And that's the problem. You want more?"

"God, there's more?"

"Listen to this. We were in Balboa waiting around for orders to come out here. Every night the crew was having liberty and if you've ever been in Balboa you know how they were living it up. One night Spaugh went ashore on his own. I had the watch and stayed aboard. Around midnight we got a message requesting the senior officer aboard to report immediately to the Port Director's office. So I left Dick Vernor in charge of the ship and went right over. They told me the police had picked up Spaugh and they were holding him on some kind of rape charge. My first reaction was 'Good! Good riddance.' But the Port Director told me I'd better go over to the police station and straighten things out. I didn't want to but I knew there was no choice. But first I came back to the ship, all the time trying to figure out a plan. I felt good about him being in the slammer but I knew I had to get him out or there'd be hell to pay.

"I decided to pull a bluff.. To do it I needed a guy I could depend on and could keep his mouth shut. Most of the crew was on liberty, living it up in Balboa. I wanted either Junior Fairlie or Moyer but they were both on liberty. I finally picked Stengele. I had him come down here in the wardroom and I told him the skipper was in a jam and had been busted and he and I had to work as a team to spring him loose. I told him to get dressed in his navy whites, find or make a Shore Patrol band for his arm, and get himself a billy club. I told him he was to accompany me as a Shore Patrol officer."

"How did he react?"

"He didn't want to do it. He was scared they'd find out and he'd be in trouble. I told him I would take responsibility for everything, including protecting him if we were caught. I finally had to order him to do as I said. He was pissed but he left and about an hour later he showed up decked out in his whites with an SP band and—would you believe it—he'd managed to get some puttees for his ankles and he had a billy club. He looked pretty convincing.

"Well, we took a taxi to the police station, which is where the jail was also, and the sergeant told us that Spaugh had been picked up in some joint, very drunk and disorderly, and supposedly had moved too fast on one of the women. She started screaming and yelling bloody murder and someone called the police. When they came she accused Spaugh of trying to rape her.

"I told the sergeant he could turn Spaugh over to us and we'd be responsible for him. I told him Spaugh would be placed in our brig pending a board of inquiry. I told him he'd probably be court-martialed and it would be better for the navy to handle the matter and keep relationships with civilian police on an even keel. I've got to hand it to Stengele, he played the part perfectly. He really looked like the Shore Patrol. The sergeant was good about it and brought Spaugh out. He looked bad, his face was flushed, his eyelids drooping, he was still drunk. But he was sober enough to realize what was happening and he was one scared ship's captain. We got him out to the taxi and brought him back to the ship."

"Did he ever say anything about it?"

"He just laughed it off. He's that type. He had no idea what Stengele and I went through to get him out of one helluva mess. His navy career was on the line."

"That's quite a story," I said. "But I guess it's history now."

"I suppose so, but the guy's not only a thief, he's a loose cannon. You never know what's going to happen next with him. He can't be trusted. Ted, I'm the executive officer. I'm second in command. We've got a great bunch of guys on this ship but already I can see it beginning to affect their morale. It's been bugging me so much a few days ago I even looked in Navy Regs about the possibility of taking over command. Under unusual circumstances it can be done. They've got it all laid out. Here, I'll show you." Jerry's law training was working at full speed. He stood up and reached for the heavy, thick book of Navy Regulations on the shelf above his desk. He found the page he was looking for and placed it on the desk in front of me. "Start here," he said, pointing, "And read these two Articles." They read:

> Article 184. It is conceivable that most unusual and extraordinary circumstances may arise in which the relief from duty of a commanding officer by a subordinate becomes necessary, either by placing him under arrest or on the sick list; but such action shall never be taken without the approval of the Navy Department or other appropriate higher authority, except when reference to such higher authority is undoubtedly impracticable because of the delay involved or for other clearly obvious reason. Such reference must set forth all facts in the case, and the reasons for the recommendation, with particular regard to the degree of urgency involved.
>
> Article 185. In order that a subordinate officer, acting upon his own initiative, may be vindicated for relieving

a commanding officer from duty, the situation must be obvious and clear, and must admit of the single conclusion that the retention of command by such commanding officer will seriously and irretrievably prejudice the public interests. The subordinate officer so acting must be next in lawful succession to command; must be unable to refer the matter to a common superior for one of the reasons set down in article 184; must be certain that the prejudicial actions of his commanding officer are not caused by secret instructions unknown to the subordinate; must have given the matter such careful consideration, and must have made such exhaustive investigation of all the circumstances, as may be practicable; and finally must be thoroughly convinced that the conclusion to relieve his commanding officer is one which a reasonable, prudent, and experienced officer would regard as a necessary consequence from the facts then determined to exist.

I didn't want to be dragged into it.

"Jerry," I said, "Even if you could prove any of those things you wouldn't have a leg to stand on. It's not as though the ship is in danger. It's wartime. Who's going to care about petty thievery on board a little subchaser, even if it is the commanding officer doing the stealing? Maybe in peacetime, but not now. There's no grounds. No way. Your own career would be at stake."

Despair was written all over his face. "I know. I know. You're right. But I had to get it off my chest. Ted, I'll tell you. I hate this ship, I hate the navy, I want no part of it. I can't wait to get transferred, get off, get out of the sight and sound of Spaugh. Dick Vernor was lucky. He hated Spaugh too but he managed to get off and away from him."

The unhappy conversation ended and for the remainder of the time Jerry was on the ship, which was almost a year, we never talked about Spaugh again. It was disquieting because I had begun to regard Spaugh as a pretty good leader and, for the most part, a good ship's captain As time passed Jerry said little, rarely talking except when necessary, although he continued to be my good mentor. A couple of times he rolled his eyes at something Spaugh had said or done, but it was all unspoken. I decided the best policy for me to follow would be to put it out of my mind and carry out my responsibilities as well as possible, leave the future up to fate, and take things as they came.

We operated out of Brisbane for 100 days, from May 8th to the middle of August 1943. A few times we patrolled the harbor entrance but most of the time we escorted ships back and forth, up and down the coast. We were kept pretty busy, with a minimum time in port for refueling and replenishing our food and water. A frequent destination was Gladstone, a coastal town about 300 miles north of Brisbane. We docked in Gladstone several times while waiting to escort ships back to Brisbane. It was a small, friendly town, a good liberty port. Some of the citizens got to know us as the "Yanks from that little ship." One or two of the crew established "relationships" with female friends whose husbands or boyfriends were away fighting the war. AWOLs in Gladstone got so frequent we held muster every morning in port. One time in town a fast-talking pet shop owner sold Jay Green and Fred Esser a wallaby for fifty pounds—an outrageous price. They brought it back to the ship and pleaded with us to keep it as a ship's pet. We foolishly gave in on condition they took full responsibility for its care and feeding. We soon discovered "Wally's" I.Q. was not very high, even for a wallaby. He was unresponsive and unhappy and wanted only to get away from anyone who came near. Three different times he jumped over the side and had to be rescued. This gave us good practice in man-overboard drills. On one of our trips to Gladstone he jumped off the ship onto a dock and headed for a grassy knoll beyond the loading area. Three crew members dropped everything and gave chase, running after him as he bounded up the knoll and disappeared. After an hour the men returned empty-handed. As a reward for their zeal

Spaugh gave the three men a couple of hours extra duty for going AWOL.

That afternoon we sailed back to Brisbane, thinking (hoping) we had seen the last of Wally. But a week later upon returning to Gladstone, no sooner had we docked than a farmer pulled up in a horse and wagon. In the back sat Wally looking as indifferent as ever. Someone had told the farmer he was off our ship. He had been keeping an eye out for us. He tried to make us think he had done us a big favor and hung around for a while until the crew collected some change and gave him a tip. Actually, we were doing him a favor. Farmers hate "roos" and wallabies because they eat grass and feed intended for their livestock.

Wally continued his sulky, unhappy existence until a few weeks later, when we were ordered to New Guinea. Crossing the Coral Sea we had made landfall and were approaching Milne Bay when Wally jumped ship for the last time. We were escorting a convoy and couldn't stop. The last we saw of him he was swimming with all his might for the palm-treed shores of New Guinea. If he made it, life had to have been better for him than on the 648.

The cockatoo that radioman Esser bought was almost as unfriendly and unresponsive as Wally, although it did allow itself to be carried on the men's shoulders. We called him "Cocky." He was supposed to talk—at least that's what Esser said the pet store man had told him. But the only sound he ever made was an occasional squawk, accompanied by a raising of his feathered crest. He did this whenever he saw a crew member he disliked, so it was rather often.

One day I was standing on the quarterdeck and Cocky half fluttered, half fell from the flying bridge, landing on my shoulder. He couldn't really fly because his wings had been clipped. I let him perch on my shoulder while listening to something Moyer, our sonarman, was telling me. Moyer suddenly stopped talking and started laughing, pointing to my chest. Cocky had plopped a big gob of cockatoo crud into my shirt pocket, in which was an open pack of cigarettes.

Speaking of cigarettes, one of the dumbest things I ever did on that ship was to start smoking. Everyone on the ship smoked. Cigarettes were plentiful and cheap—you could buy a carton at ship's store for ninety cents. A few months after coming aboard I thought smoking would be good for relaxation and help occupy the time. There was a camaraderie—a bonding—when you lit up a cigarette with someone. Everyone else was smoking, so why not? It didn't matter that I was born with a sensitive chest and a bagful of allergies. With my history of childhood asthma I should have thought twice about smoking, but in those days I didn't think of a lot of things. Smoking was natural for everyone out there. At first I didn't even enjoy the sensation of inhaling—it made me dizzy—but, rashly, having to prove something, I insidiously got used to it until it became a habit that lasted off and on for twenty years. I finally broke it but it wasn't easy and to this day I regret having smoked at all.

During those three months in Australia we operated with several Australian corvettes and motor launches on escort trips to and from Gladstone and Curtis Bay. On one of these voyages ML 429 picked up an underwater echo and we stood by to assist. We ended up making a mousetrap attack but nothing resulted. The 429's echo proved to be a false alarm. On another voyage we made a full-fledged attack that lasted more than an hour. Our sonar had picked up a distinct, sharp echo of an underwater target and the corvette HMAS Vendette ordered us to stay with it while the convoy proceeded on its way. Readings of successive ranges and bearings indicated the underwater object was moving. Spaugh called the crew to general quarters and we mounted an attack with our mousetraps. Two underwater explosions resulted, which meant we had hit something because they would explode only on contact.

We followed the mousetraps with a full-pattern depth charge attack. The charges exploded at their depth settings and we waited for some sign of a hit. All we got was a good-sized air bubble and a wisp of oil on the surface. Later inquiry dispelled any notion that we had hit a submarine because official records showed that no Jap subs were operating within 500 miles of our location at the time. To this day I think of the sharpness and clarity of that echo, wondering what we hit, and can only conclude that it was a sunken steel hull that, in our excitement, we thought was "moving."

Another incident while we were in Australia is worth mentioning. On July 23, 1943, while in Gladstone, we were ordered to proceed as quickly as possible to Heron Islet to rescue survivors (if any) from an RAAF Anson medium bomber that had crashed, either on or near the island. Heron Islet was about forty miles east by northeast from Gladstone, one of thousands of islands that dot the Great Barrier Reef. Stretchers and extra blankets were loaded aboard and we took off at high speed. After two and a half hours we spotted the island, a low, flat atoll, green with palms and tropical growth, fringed with a sparkling white beach. There appeared to be no sign of life, nor any sign of an airplane. The island appeared to be uninhabited. In the bright sunlight it looked like a tropical paradise. Spaugh maneuvered the ship to a point about a hundred yards off the beach and anchored. Everyone wanted to be in on the rescue, but that being impossible, Spaugh selected five men: Beanblossom, Moyer, Touhy, Swett, and Hulse. They launched the wherry and tied both life rafts behind it. We watched as they rowed in with the rafts in tow, beached, secured the wherry and rafts, and disappeared into the green of the island. Twenty minutes later Hulse appeared on the beach and semaphored that they had found the plane and were starting recovery work.

After an hour or so they reappeared, bearing two stretchers, each with a man who appeared lifeless. Leaving

Beanblossom on the beach with the two lifeless forms, they went back and returned with two more. A final trip produced a fifth body. After several minutes of preparation on the beach they began paddling back, towing the two rafts, one containing two bodies and the other three bodies. Once aboard and everything secured, we got underway and proceeded back to Gladstone at high speed. Three of the flyers were dead. The two still surviving were unconscious and badly injured, one of them with his leg almost severed below the knee. Beanblossom tended them as tenderly and carefully as though they were his brothers.

We arrived back in Gladstone around midnight and a couple of ambulances took the flyers away. We learned a day or two later that one of the two didn't make it. The other man recovered and in 1995 Beanblossom told me that for many years afterward he received Christmas cards from him and his wife.

Today a vacation and resort company operates scuba diving and snorkeling vacations on Heron Island. At the time we were there we had little time to appreciate the pristine beauty of this magnificent little atoll.

The duty up and down the east coast of Australia was very good on-the-job training for me. Jerry passed along much of what he had learned at SCTC about piloting and celestial navigation and several times Spaugh let me practice docking and maneuvering the ship in tight spaces. I established good relationships with the enlisted men. Their skills as sailors were impressive. Rice, SM/2c, could do semaphore and work a blinker light faster than many regular navy men on bigger ships. No one could keep our diesel engines running like Fairlie, despite the lack of spare parts. George Green, coxswain, straight off his family's farm in upstate New York, was highly skilled in marlinespike seamanship. He fashioned monkey fists, fenders, and other things out of rope, including a bit of macramé to decorate one of the pilot house ports. Moyer on sonar, Esser in the radio shack, Fagan the cook—they didn't come any better than these. The yeoman, Vic Beck, was indisputably the best yeoman in the navy. He knew every detail, every navy form (and there were hundreds), every protocol. In addition he was a great typist. He would bring official letters to us for signing and they were always letter perfect and neat.

Seasickness was no longer a problem. My sea legs were steadier, even on days when it was rough and we took green water over the bow. I continued with the correspondence course in navigation and practiced taking sextant readings and figuring our position. I studied the Submarine Chaser Manual, a restricted navy publication containing vital information about submarine attack, anti-aircraft defense, escort, patrol, shiphandling, engineering, communications, and many other things necessary to self-improvement as a watch officer. The three months of cruising up and down the Australian coast turned into my personal training program. The experience gave me a big boost in confidence. By the middle of August, when we headed north to New Guinea, I felt comfortable with my job and my niche in the navy. To top it off, a letter arrived dated July 16, 1943, from BuPers, making my promotion to the rank of lieutenant (jg) official.

Australia 93

A few of the ship's company, July 1943

Front row left to right: F.J.Stengele EM2c; Lt.(jg) P.S.Spaugh, C.O.;
    C.O.Keltner MoMM2c; R.J.Dreyer S1c; G.H.Green S2c
Second row left to right: V.F.Beck Y3c; J.Q.Green GM2c; L.George GM2c
    T.W.Esser RM1c; R.Newman RM3c; Lt.(jg) G.M.Lively, Exec.Officer
Third row left to right: L.J.Carnago S1c; A.Kennedy F3c; R.C.Beebe GM2c;
    R.F.Fagan SC3c; R.D.VanKirk S2c
Top, sitting: H.V.Rice Sn2c

New Guinea

On August 18, 1943, we left Townsville to escort a convoy of four APcs and a navy tanker across the Coral Sea to Milne Bay, New Guinea. Ships and planes from the U.S. were finally arriving in numbers and General MacArthur and the Seventh Fleet were in a position to take the offensive in the Pacific war. Never aware of the grand plans and strategy, we simply accepted that we were a small part of MacArthur's game plan to return to the Philippines and that New Guinea was a natural stepping-stone toward this goal. Little did I realize I would be in New Guinea for three-quarters of a year before returning to Australia as the new commanding officer of SC 648.

New Guinea, the second largest island in the world, is shaped like a gigantic bird, its head pointing westward and positioned as though it's about to devour Halmaherah Island. From its head the bird's body sprawls eastward some 1,600 miles, ending in a clefted tail formed by Milne Bay, a great, 5-mile-wide bight that runs 26 miles into the land. Surrounded by mountainous jungles that grow down to the water, most of Milne Bay is very deep until it ends at Gili Gili, an alluvial plain where, at the time of the war, there was a big coconut plantation operated by Lever Brothers.

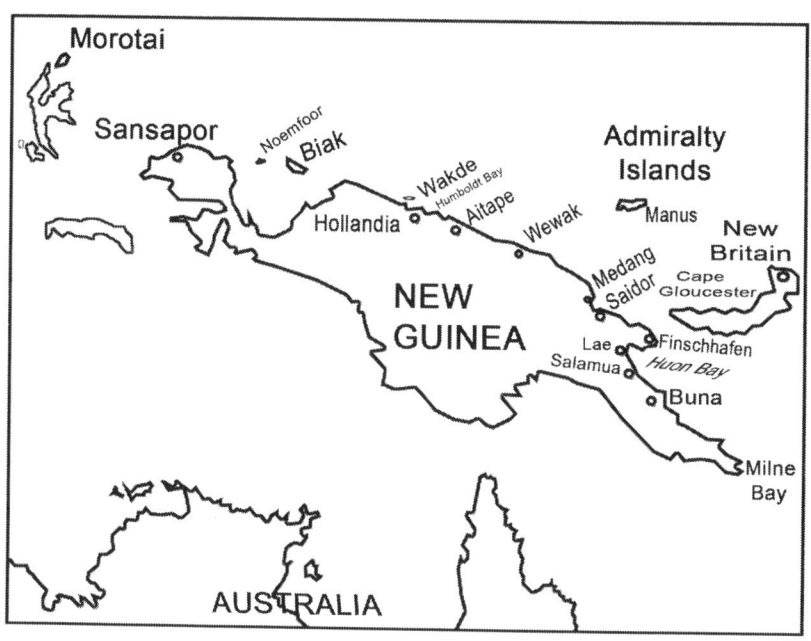

Map showing area where SC 648 operated for more than nine months

When we arrived at Milne Bay it was teeming with ships and activity, having been established a year or so previously by U.S. Army Engineers and a company of Australian infantry. It was a valuable Allied resource, providing anchorage for vast numbers of ships, shore facilities for staging areas, and a strategic airfield. Milne Bay was to be our "home," our "marina," our so-called liberty port for the next several months.

No time was wasted putting us to work. We had hardly replenished our fuel, water, and food before being ordered to escort a group of five LCIs to Oro Bay, about 200 miles along the New Guinea coast, 20 miles east of Buna, where troops were still heavily engaged in jungle fighting. At Oro we waited for the LCIs to disgorge reinforcement troops onto the beach and then escorted them back to Milne Bay, where we nested with several other subchasers alongside the USS *Rigel*, a repair ship that, at the time, served as Admiral Barbey's headquarters. For three weeks we plied back and forth to Oro, Morobe, and Buna, escorting various landing craft—LCTs, LCMs, LCIs, and LSTs. Sometimes the LCTs and LCMs would straggle or get too far out of formation and we'd have to round them up. We went to general quarters when enemy planes were spotted or reported in the vicinity, but since they were usually out of range we seldom opened fire. One day at Morobe we scrambled to general quarters when we received a radio message that nine medium bombers and an undetermined number of fighters were headed our way. A few minutes later we spotted the bombers, too high and out of range, but then a couple of fighter planes swooped in and all the ships including ours opened fire. There were no hits and as quickly as they flew in, they were gone.

The "Black Gang"

Left to right: Kennedy F3C, Keltner MoMM2C, Fairlie MM1C, Stengele EM2C

For three weeks the back-and-forth trips from Milne to points west continued with barely enough time in port to refuel, replenish water and food, and get ourselves ready to go out again. Sometimes the weather would get very rough, with green seas breaking constantly over the bow. The result would be a lot of wet bedding and general discomfort in our living quarters—particularly the crews' quarters. We weren't in port long enough to air bedding properly or do our laundry. We looked pretty scruffy during those times.

On one of these trips we were returning to Milne Bay independently, cruising at 12 knots about 5,000 yards off the coast. The enemy had been driven from this section of New Guinea several months before. It was one of those quiet, idyllic days with no breeze and the water as smooth as glass. I stood on the flying bridge with Spaugh, who was studying the coastline intently through his binoculars.

"Hey, take a look," he said, pointing to a spot on the coast and handing me the binoculars. "Man, does that look inviting or does that look inviting?"

Looking through the binoculars I saw a little stretch of white beach with some thatched roofs behind it. It was a native New Guinea village.

"Pretty nice," I said.

"Know what? We're gonna take a look." Leaning into the voice tube he called down, "Come right, all engines one-third."

The ship slowed perceptibly and we swung around until we were facing the shore in the direction of the village.

"Steady as you go," Spaugh sang out through the tube.

He said, "We've been going pretty hot and heavy lately and the guys need a break. This'll give 'em a chance to relax a little and see something different. God a'mighty, there's no liberty for anyone here and this might be just enough to take their minds off their problems and help morale."

I had to admire him for his audacity. We had no idea what might be there in that village, even though we had good reason to believe the Japs had all been cleared out. Was he taking an unnecessary chance, or did he know something no one else knew? Anyone's guess. No hesitation though. Spaugh was like that—spontaneous, adventurous, unafraid, and curious.

Word was passed and soon everyone was topside, looking toward the shore, talking about the beach and the village. Spaugh stationed a couple of men in the bow to take soundings. The water was crystal clear, the bottom sandy. Slowly approaching, we saw several typical native huts with their thatched roofs, although there seemed to be no signs of life. We couldn't see any natives at all. Had the village been abandoned, a victim of the war?

We anchored about 50 yards offshore. Spaugh asked for a show of hands to see how many men wanted to swim into the beach and take a look around. About half of them raised their hands. Jerry said he'd stay with the ship so I went, along with Spaugh and a dozen or so men. Stripping down to our cutoffs, we plunged in. The water was warm and beautiful and it was an easy swim to the beach, a beautiful setting fringed with palm trees shading thatched-roofed huts, a travel agent's dream.

As we emerged from the water a big black fellow with a bushy head of hair appeared, greeting us with a wide grin, his teeth filed down almost to his gums and blackened from chewing betel nuts. He said something and pointed to the huts but we couldn't understand him. We walked through an open space faced by the huts. People were lounging inside but making no effort to come out. The big fellow pointed to a larger hut with its roof only half covered. After much back and forth questioning and gestures we got the idea that it was a hospital. We stood around a few minutes, not knowing what to do. The people inside their huts seemed so listless we couldn't figure out what was wrong.

Just then an Australian major neatly dressed in khaki shorts strolled up. The big black fellow retreated to one of the huts.

"I say, Yanks, who's in charge here?" the major asked. Spaugh introduced himself.

"You shouldn't be here." The major spoke in even tones. "This village is under quarantine. They all have hookworm. You can't stay here. You must go back to your ship right now." He looked down at our bare feet.

"And when you get back to your ship you should wash your feet thoroughly with soap and water and put something on them to kill the parasite. It's here in the sand and it gets into your body through your feet. Use alcohol or an insecticide, something to kill the larvae."

As we began our retreat to the water the major said, "Oh, by the way lads, you won't know you've got the disease for seven years. It takes that long to gestate and manifest itself." He stood there, smiling.

So much for our exploration party. Even Spaugh was subdued. When we got back aboard no time was wasted doing exactly what the major had said, and thoroughly. As far as I know no one ever contracted the disease.

Of the various discomforts aboard a subchaser few were as invasive and irritating as the hordes of Blattidae—the common cockroach. Our ship was no exception, and throughout the entire time I was aboard SC 648 we encountered and fought these filthy pests in varying degrees, depending upon local circumstances. While I was writing Splinter Fleet a good friend of mine, Al Angellini, who had served aboard SC 744, sent me an anonymous poem that, in its outlandishness, gets to the very nugget of the cockroach problem aboard ship. Good enough to use in Splinter Fleet, it is repeated here to make the point:

Hi'ya Cockroach!

T'rou' da bilges went da cockroach, t'rough' da bilges, t'rou' da galley.
Found dey food and found dey feasting, t'rou' da galley, t'rou' da lockers,
'Til we catchem wid da Flit gun, den dey take da Flit gun from us,
Move us over at da table, holler "Guts!" and pound da table,
Claim dey cannot eat dat moose dung! So went sailors t'rou' da bilges,
T'rou' da bilges, t'rou' da galley. Locked demselves inside da lockers,
Barricade demselves wid broomsticks,
Lived on scraps da bugs would t'row dem,
While da cockroach, unmolested,
Took command and gave da orders, and da Navy was no wiser.
So at night we roam da bilges. T'rou' da bilges, t'rou' da galley,
And at night you hear us scratching, t'rou' da bilges, t'rou' da galley.

—Anonymous

All ships, including the largest, most deluxe cruise ships, have to fight this wily, hardened invader, one of planet Earth's most enduring species. Cockroaches thrive in the tropics and quickly infest ships after being brought aboard in food crates. If left uncontrolled they flourish in ships' galleys where there's an abundance of food. With little control under wartime conditions our galley—hot, humid, and no bigger than a walk-in closet—was cockroach heaven and it was there that they thrived and multiplied. Ridding ourselves of the pests was a problem because we had such little time to wash clothes, fight rust, make repairs, and dry out bedding before being sent out again. The cockroaches would have to wait.

Sometimes we'd be at the table eating and a cockroach would walk along the table, flagrantly waving its antennae as if to say "Here I am, what are you going to do about it?" It happened so frequently we generally did nothing as long as he didn't get too close to our plate. There were nights when I'd go down into the galley for a cup of coffee before going on watch. I'd grope my way down the ladder into the after compartment, work my way into the galley and close the galley door before turning on the light. Instantly, thousands of cockroaches under my feet, others on the counter, scurried for cover. The sound of their rustling could actually be heard over the loud hum of the engines.

It would be easy to blame Fagan, our ship's cook, for the cockroaches, but they were as unstoppable as a burst water pipe. He kept the galley as clean as possible under difficult conditions. Fagan never complained. The officers were as much to blame as anyone. We'd hear an enlisted man say something about "the goddammed cockroaches" and figure if he weren't bitching about roaches he'd be bitching about something else. Once George Green found brown stains on his dress whites, caused by cockroaches. He decided he'd had enough.

George Green S2C

"I'll fix those S.O.B.s," he announced to fellow crew members. Whether he was referring to the cockroaches or to the officers is not clear but it doesn't matter. Gathering several live roaches and picking a time when no one was around, Green planted them in the wardroom—in the bunks, behind the desks, in the head. Back in the crew's quarters he rubbed his hands and cackled, "Guess that'll get some action."

It did. Only a few days later when we got into port Spaugh had the ship quarantined. Everyone had to get off so it could be disinfected with an anti-pest bomb. The procedure took about four hours, after which the ship was free from cockroaches—for a few days. But it wasn't long before the critters—like the brooms of the Sorcerer's Apprentice—returned as audacious and independent as ever. The cycle repeated itself half a dozen times during my tenure. I never knew that George Green planted the roaches in the wardroom until fifty years later, when I visited his brother Jay in upstate New York and we swapped stories and memories.

The galley was the domain of Robert F. Fagan, ship's cook. Tall, thin, pale, and stripped to the waist, his torso glistening with sweat, Fagan doggedly fixed three meals a day seven days a week for the twenty-seven men of the 648. We seldom saw Fagan topside. He never complained once during his two-year stint on the ship even though he was chronically seasick. In some ways seasickness was actually a relief for him when, too sick to cook, he could crap out in his bunk.. No one complained because everyone liked Fagan and his cooking. In rough seas Swett or Stengele would fill in for him and we'd eat cold sandwiches and little else, but it was accepted.

Fagan's job as ship's cook was daunting. It wasn't so bad while we were in Brisbane because we were able to get fresh eggs, milk, vegetables, and meat, the latter often being Australian mutton, which few of the crew would eat. But when we got to New Guinea our staples were dehydrated milk, powdered potatoes, Spam, and canned vegetables. Sailors like to eat well and will go to great lengths to get good food. On our many forays for food supplies we learned our way around depots and how to deal with supply sergeants who were frequently overbearing toward lowly ships like subchasers. We were forever trying to better the ship's humdrum diet. Luxuries like ice cream, American beef, fresh produce, or less common foods required flattery, bartering, promises of reward, bribery, or—as a last resort—thievery.

It was during these work parties that I came to know Fagan as another unforgettable guy. He was born and raised in Wilmington, Delaware; his mother died when he was very young and he lived with his alcoholic father until he finished high school. He was smart and got good grades but when he was accepted by the University of Delaware, his father wouldn't let him go, saying he'd supported him for eighteen years and he should get out and earn for himself. Tough and tenacious, Fagan found a job in a restaurant. By the time war broke out he had a steady girlfriend and had saved enough money to get married. But "her parents were against it," he told me. "They thought I wasn't good enough for her."

Like most ship's cooks, thick-skinned and deaf to insults, Fagan enjoyed standing in the galley door during mealtimes, his arms folded, trading barbs with the crew as they ate. "Junior" Fairlie, MoMM1C would start it.

Fairlie: "Jeez, Fagan, this is the third time in a week we've had shit-on-a-shingle."

Fagan: "Hey, why don't you write your congressman? Oh, I forgot. Someone's gotta teach you to write first."

Fairlie: "Yeah, I think I will write. I'll ask him to get you a transfer."

Fagan: "Great. You'd be doin' me a favor. I've been trying to get a transfer ever since I came aboard. I mean ever since you came aboard.

Fairlie: "I'll have him get you Ship's Cook First Class on a garbage barge."

Fagan: "Yeah, and you can be my motor mac."

Fairlie: "Good. At least the chow would be better'n this."

Fagan: "Hey, you wanna cook? Here, take my apron. I'll trade my job for yours any time you want."

Fairlie: "Aaaah, forget it, Fagan, these guys don't know the difference. They couldn't tell a cow's ass from horse cock anyway."

At which the diners would turn on Fairlie and Fagan had the last laugh.

The crew ate in two shifts in the after compartment, followed by the officers, also in the after compartment. The men rotated duty as mess cooks. The only difference between officers' fare and the crew's was that Fagan gave the officers cloth napkins. We never criticized the food and if we liked a dish we'd tell him so. We liked Fagan. He worked hard and he was intelligent. He made nothing special just for us, but once in a while he'd save us extra helpings of pie or cake. The pies were made from canned peaches, cherries, and pineapple but Fagan made them tasty, with crisp, flaky crusts. Crisco was one of his staples

Maintaining sanitation not only in the galley but everywhere on the 648 was not easy. Tropical heat and humidity, a lack of time to clean and air bedding properly, the limited supply of fresh water for laundry and bathing, the crowded conditions—all these things added up to not much more than squalor. More than once I woke up in the middle of the night bathed in so much sweat it formed a puddle under my body. We were at sea and all I could do was turn back the top sheet and let the bottom dry out as much as possible between watches. Under such conditions it's a wonder we didn't contract a serious disease but most of us stayed healthy despite our unsanitary, unhealthy, and uncomfortable environment.

When Fagan was transferred back to the States in June 1944 we had three successive ship's cooks while I was still aboard but none of them were as good as Fagan. Despite his bouts with seasickness he was a very good cook and shipmate. The same men who sullied him for so long and so unmercifully were even worse with his successors, taunting them with remarks such as "Wish we had Fagan back" and "As a cook you're an amateur compared to Fagan." One of the new cooks lost his temper and threatened a man with a knife. We had to transfer him off the ship.

For nine months, from early September 1943 to May 1944, we operated along the coast of New Guinea between Milne Bay, Morobe Bay, and Buna. On September 3 and 4 we were part of the task force in the landing at Lae in the Huon Gulf. Our role was to escort two APCs and fourteen LCTs from Milne Bay to Morobe, on to Buna, thence to Huon Gulf and Lae. At Morobe the task force was raided by nine medium bombers and thirty-three unidentified fighters. Though the planes kept their distance and flew largely out of range the entire convoy opened fire, a deafening barrage that lasted for thirty minutes. No planes were hit but we gained experience on the 40 mm gun, range-finding, leading the target, and holding fire when target was out of range. After experiencing several skirmishes like this I realized an awful lot of ammunition

The crew clusters at rail, awaiting arrival of long-overdue mail.

Capt. Spaugh carries mail bags to quarterdeck.

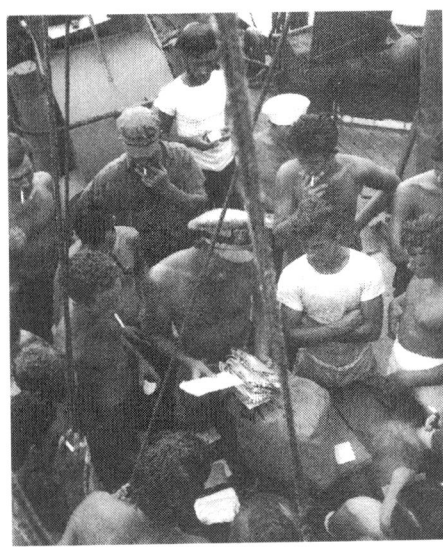
Spaugh distributes mail

Reading mail

was wasted by ships who fired too soon or too late, but particularly when the target was out of range.

We operated in a relatively small area of New Guinea from Milne Bay to the Huon Gulf. We cruised endlessly back and forth from Milne Bay to Morobe to Finschhafen to Lae to Buna, back to Finschhafen, down to Milne, back to Huon, repeat, repeat. We escorted cargo ships, floating dry docks, oilers, luggers, transports, landing craft, just about any kind of ship you can name. The duty was dull in good weather, rigorous in bad, but always continuous and relentless. No sooner would we get into port than we'd take on water, food, and fuel and go out again, sometimes in a matter of hours. Too often there was no time to launder, air bedding, or tend to routine maintenance. Rust broke out everywhere, spotting the depth charge racks, ammo lockers, ground tackle, and mousetrap rails like acne on a kid's face. Saltwater stains encrusting the hull and barnacles along the waterline gave proof of the need for drydocking. The ship looked more like a tired old fishing trawler than a proud little U.S. Navy warship.

Morale often dipped. Mail was always weeks behind, always following, never catching up. Bedding was either wet or damp—always foul smelling. Dirty clothes and laundry had to wait. Body odor and smell of urine permeated the crews quarters. Topside the sharp, acrid smell of diesel fumes was sickening. A semi-permanent miasma enveloped the ship. The only ones who were happy were the cockroaches gorging themselves in the galley and making love around the clock. The diesel engines balked. They needed new liners that never came. Plugs, lifters, and ordinary spare parts were scarce or nonexistent. Junior Fairlie kept them running with wire and duct tape, and to this day I don't know how he did it.

We were a tiny pawn on General MacArthur's chessboard and he was moving us and all the other players in a grand strategy about which we knew nothing. The ship's log reflects this during and after the invasion at Lae, New Guinea. Our part in that operation was limited to escorting and patrolling and at no time were we very near the beach.

> 9/4/43 Invasion force passes. 0618 Destroyers bombard beach. 0625 Patrolling off Red Beach. 1430 Last LCT off beach, convoy forming up. 1515 proceeding out of Huon Gulf. 2230 passed Kakara Is. Close aboard to port.
>
> 9/5/43 0155 Convoy laying to off Morobe Bay. 0415 Underway. 1452 Entering Buna Bay. 1545 Moored. 1754 Underway departing Buna Bay. 1800 forming up with SC734, SC745 & SC637 bound for Morobe.
>
> 9/6/43 0120 Anchored in Morobe Bay. 0835 Underway, bound for Porlock Hbr departing Morobe Bay with SC637 and SC745. 0945 off Morobe Bay awaiting convoy. 1115 Joined by convoy of 7 LST, 4 DD & 2 SC enroute to Buna. 1915 Laying to off Buna #1 buoy. 2115 Underway.

9/7/43 Steaming as before. 0150 and 0210 joined by SC 698 & 637. Bound for Morobe. 0620 passed Buna #1 buoy, joined by SC 742. 0939 entering Morobe Bay. 1308 Red Alert. 1408 All Clear, no planes sighted. 1606 Anchored. 1705 Red Alert, 1706 Opened fire on enemy aircraft. 1707 underway. 1710 Ceased fire. 1735 Returned to anchorage. No damage. No results.

9/8/43 Anchored as before. 1048 Red Alert. 1100 All Clear, nothing sighted. 1142 Red Alert. 1158 All clear nothing sighted. 1400 Yellow Alert. 1445 All clear. 1749 Underway departing Morobe, joined SC 698 (SOPA) SC 637, SC 749 acting as escort to LST 67 bound for Buna Bay. 2215 Commenced raining; visibility dropped. Lost sight of convoy. 2250 Convoy in sight.

9/9/43 Steaming as before. 0120 Rain commenced. 0130 Lost sight of convoy. 0150 Visibility zero. 0230 Visibility clearing. No sight of convoy. 0328 Sighted lights, apparently Buna. 0330 Laying to to identify position. Rain ceased. 0335 Area discovered to be Oro Bay, changed course accordingly. 0725 Entering Buna Bay. 0748 Anchored.

9/10/43 Anchored as before. 1108 Underway, laying to off #1 buoy awaiting convoy. 1150 Six LCIs headed toward Red Beach. 1210 Underway to escort LCIs in company with DDs Lamson, Drayton, Reid and Mugford. 0300 Patrolling off Red Beach in Huon Gulf awaiting return of six LCIs.

9/11/43 Patrolling as before. 0110 LCIs off beach, joining up. 0115 underway, bound for Morobe. 0725 Entering Morobe Bay. 0750 Anchored. 0913 Red Alert. 0952 All Clear, no enemy sighted.

9/12/43 Anchored as before. 0841 Underway to escort 2 LSTs to Buna in company with SC742 and 698. 1315 G.Q. Sighted enemy plane flying low and close to convoy. 1217 Opened fire. 1320 Planes scattered. Ceased firing. No casualties, no results. 1327 Secured from GQ. 1705 Anchored in Buna Bay. 1753 Underway with SC742, bound for Morobe.

9/13/43 0055 Anchored in Morobe Bay. 0958 Red Alert. 1012 All Clear, nothing sighted. 1401 Red Alert.

1404 All Clear nothing sighted. 1920 Red Alert. 1953 All Clear, nothing sighted. 1005 Red Alert. 2013 Underway. Heavy 90mm fire on beach. No planes sighted. 2110 Secured from GQ nothing sighted and no casualties. 2113 Anchored in Morobe Bay.

9/14/43 Anchored as before. 0825 Red Alert. 0842 All Clear, nothing sighted. 0937 SC699 moored alongside. 1140 Red Alert. 1145 All clear nothing sighted. 2124 Red Alert, AA firing on beach. 2135 Sighted 2 enemy planes. 2200 All clear. 2225 Red Alert. 2238 All clear. 2301 Red alert. 2328 All clear, nothing sighted.

9/15/43 Anchored as before. 0851 SC 699 underway. 1004 Underway various courses and speeds transiting Morobe River. 1026 Moored portside to water dock at PT base Morobe. 1127 Underway, winding ship to transit Morobe River, screws touching bottom. 1128 Transiting Morobe R. and Bay. 1230 Anchored in Morobe Bay.

That last entry is the logbook's version of an audacious sortie by Captain Spaugh up the Morobe River in search of fresh water. No ships had ever ventured up the river and when Spaugh told Jim Forrestal, skipper of SC 699, that he was going to try it Forrestal shook his head, unbelieving, saying "You fool, you'll run her aground." But we went anyway and after a half-hour meandering up the fetid, narrow, river, we arrived at a PT base with a water dock to which we tied up and took on fresh water after being told we'd never get potable water from the river itself. Getting the ship turned around to head back was touch-and-go because the river was so narrow, but Spaugh was in his element, geeing and hawing the ship in its turning maneuvers, scraping the bottom and churning up mud in great quantities. When we arrived back in Morobe Bay the officers on the other ships just shook their heads, muttering, "That damn crazy Spaugh."

> 9/16/43 Anchored as before. 1156 Underway, bound for Red Beach with SC 749 and SC 742 and Apc 6 as escort to 7 LCTs and 9 LCVPs. 2240 Convoy goes to Red Beach. 0310 Tracer fire directed toward LCTs. They returned fire. 2320 GQ. Heavy gunfire. 2350 Secured from GQ. No results, no damage.
>
> 9/17/43 Patrolling as before. 0230 Convoy forming up, four DD joined convoy. 1230 Entering Morobe Hbr. 1353 Anchored in Morobe Hbr. 1738 Yellow Alert. 1753 Secured, nothing sighted.
>
> 9/18/43 Anchored as before. 1100 Red Alert. 1110 All clear, nothing sighted. 1534 Underway joined by SC698 to escort 6 LCT to Buna.
>
> 9/21/43 Steaming as before. 1315 Patroling in Huon Gulf off Red & George Beaches. 1757 GQ Sighted enemy planes. Commenced firing. Several bombs dropped with no apparent damage. 1800 Ceased firing. Planes beyond range. No results. 1822 All clear, secured from GQ. 1845 Steaming to Morobe in company with SC 698 & SC 703 as escorts to LST squad.209.
>
> 9/22/43 Steaming as before. 0232 Anchored in Morobe Bay. 1235 Underway departing Morobe enroute to Scarlet Beach with SC 703 & SC 742 as escort to X Squad 20. 1545 DD 367 DD 368 DD 366 and DD 389 joined convoy. 2210 Heavy fire by DDs on starboard beam. Target invisible. 2215 Patrolling off Scarlet Beach. 2335 DDs ceased firing.

D-day at Finschhafen, New Guinea, was September 22, when Australian troops were put ashore in a full-scale amphibious landing. The 648 and other subchasers escorted the landing vessels to a point about 1,500 yards from the beach. There was no enemy counterfire.

> 10/4/43 Anchored as before. 0205 Underway on rescue mission to pick up survivors of DD 391 in company with SC 637 SC 734 SC 703. 0330 in vicinity of sinking. Sighted several empty life rafts. 1200 Secured from

search, steaming independently. 1905 Anchored in Buna Bay.

DD 391 was the destroyer USS Henley, torpedoed and sunk by Japanese submarine RO-108 with the loss of several of her crewmen. For more than eight hours we and three other subchasers searched the area without finding any survivors.

> 10/6/43 Anchored as before. 0555 Underway to rendezvous with convoy of 4 LSTs in company with SC 981 SC 703 DD 364 DD 369 & DD 378. 2200 Patrolling off Lae, LSTs proceeding into beach.
> 10/7/43 Patrolling as before. 0245 LSTs off beach, resumed escorting of convoy to Buna Bay. 1805 Departing convoy. 1914 Anchored in Buna Bay.
> 10/11/43 Anchored as before. 0656 Underway to join convoy to Lae. Escort to 4 LSTs in company with DD 367 DD 389 and DD 364 and SC 703 and SC 981. 2205 Patrolling off Lae beach awaiting LSTs while they're beached.
> 10/17/43 Anchored as before. 0820 Returned to Buna Bay, no convoy in sight. 1005 Underway. Air raid. Enemy planes overhead. Three planes (unidentified) downed. 1035 Secured from GQ. No damage to any ships present. 1424 Anchored in Buna Bay.

The entry indicates three unidentified planes shot down. My recollection of this incident is that one plane definitely was downed and a second disappeared beyond the hills with smoke streaming from its fuselage. The third plane streaked away. Our gunners were positive we had scored hits on all three and pressed the captain to claim credit for the one that hit water. Spaugh, also convinced, went ashore to put in his claim, even though several other ships in the bay had also fired at the planes. He returned crestfallen. The planes shot down were our own, not enemy planes. No one talked about it after that.

A week or so after this unfortunate incident we returned to Milne Bay, where for the first time in several months we caught up with laundry, mail, engine repairs, painting, and general ship's maintenance. In the mail was a notice from BuPers that my officer classification had been changed from O-V(S) (Ordnance Volunteer Specialist) to D-V(G) (Deck Officer Volunteer General). It was a minor detail but one that gave me great satisfaction because it was written confirmation of my qualifications as a watch officer and it severed for good any connection with the Bureau of Ordnance. We stayed in Milne Bay almost two weeks, repairing, painting, laundering, and renewing food and supplies. A few men left the ship, replaced by new men reporting for duty. John Hulse, QM/2c, plank owner (one of the 648's original crew) was sent stateside for reassignment

Bill Touhy, BM/1c, was transferred to SC 748. I never saw or heard about him again. Richard Van Kirk, S/2c, reported aboard for duty. Van Kirk later became QM 3/c under my command, a steady, dependable youngster called "Guava" by everyone because of an outlandish story he once told about how cats wandering under guava trees would quickly perish of diarrhea. Delbert Firestine, EM/1c, of Cleveland, Ohio, was detached for hospitalization. He suffered from very flat feet, for which he was subsequently given a medical discharge. Firestine was older than most of the crew, intelligent and capable. As a civilian he had worked several years on railroad signal systems.

William Pfirter, EM/3c, reported aboard for duty. Pfirter was an electrician's mate who had several years experience in submarine duty and appeared to be an ideal replacement for Firestine. After a month aboard the 648, however, he requested a transfer back to submarine duty, giving as his reason that he "felt safer" on a submarine. Failing several attempts to dissuade him, we gave him his transfer. Years later I learned from Stengele the real reason Pfirter wanted off the 648. It was because he planned to make a career in the navy and he didn't think service on a subchaser (the Donald Duck Navy) would look good on his service record.

On November 13th we were back up in Buna to continue where we had left off, escorting ships to and from Lae, Finschaven, Morobe, and Buna. A week later Allen E. Hagmann, MoMM/1c, was transferred to SC 699. Hagmann, another plank owner of the 648, was a nice enough kid but made himself unpopular with several of the crewmen for his poker-playing prowess. His transfer proved deadly. Five months later the 699 was struck by a Kamikaze during the landing operation at Biak. Hagmann, who had just emerged from the engine room to take a look topside, was struck and killed instantly.

On November 24th we again returned to Milne Bay, where we remained until December 13th. While there our roster changed, with the additions of Fred G. Atherton, S/2c, Cletus Orville Keltner, F/3c, and Arnett Gale Cox, S/2c. After three weeks in Milne we went up to Buna only to have our port shaft disconnect. Back we went to Milne for repair. Finally, on December 23, we once again returned to Buna just in time to join Seventh Amphib, preparing for a landing of the First Marine Division at Cape Gloucester on New Britain.

The landing was made on Christmas Day without any major hitches. There was little opposition from the enemy. On the next day the 648 brought five LSTs over from Buna and escorted them into the beach. According to Samuel Eliot Morison in his definitive History of United States Naval Operations in World War II, the Cape Gloucester operation was unnecessary, since General MacArthur had a clear passage through Vitiaz Strait to the Admiralties and Hollandia. But he admits having the advantage of hindsight. Overkill was preferable to unpleasant surprise. My recollection of Cape Gloucester is one of pouring rain that never seemed to stop. Uncomfortable as we were on our little spitkit, it was ten times worse for those marines on the beach and in the jungle.

We continued operating in the triangle formed by Buna, the Huon Gulf, and Cape Gloucester, and there was little to relieve the monotony. Most of the duty was that of escorting slow, cumbersome vessels like floating dry docks, oilers, water barges, LCTs, and similar vessels.

One day we saw something in the water that looked interesting enough to investigate. It was debris from a Japanese plane that had been shot down a day or two previously—the remains of a life jacket, a seat cushion, and other bits of flotsam. Jim Moyer, sonarman, was our best swimmer and he volunteered to jump in and grapple around for anything of interest. In less than two minutes he held up an object that turned out to be a wallet and everyone gathered around for a look. In the wallet there was a picture of a young Japanese woman holding a child, with some Japanese writing on the reverse side. A few pieces of paper currency and a couple of scraps of paper with Japanese scribbling were also in the wallet.

When we got back to Finschhafen later in the day Spaugh notified the port director of our find and this was acknowledged with a message saying someone from ONI (Office of Naval Intelligence) would come to take a look. There being no available dock space we anchored a mile or so offshore in Langemak Bay, a body of water partially exposed to the sea and notorious for its heavy swells. Ships at anchor in Langemak rolled side-to-side in slow, undulating rhythm. We got accustomed to it. Sometimes it was almost pleasant to lie in your bunk rocking back and forth like a baby in his cradle.

Next morning a motor launch pulled alongside and a nattily dressed lieutenant (jg) came aboard. Facing the colors and saluting smartly, he introduced himself as a member of ONI. His dress and bearing were in startling contrast to our laid-back grunginess. He wore a tie (not since leaving the States had I seen one) on a crisply starched shirt and his khaki trousers were neatly pressed. He was a Nisei, a second-generation Japanese American, undoubtedly pressed into service for his fluency in the Japanese language. We conducted him below to the wardroom and pointed to the wallet where we had laid it on the desk.

He sat in the chair looking at the wallet.

"Have you looked inside it?" he asked.

"Well, yes," Spaugh replied, "We took a look at it."

The lieutenant shook his head. "No one should touch something like this until we've had a chance to examine it. Those are the rules," he said as he bent to look more closely.

Spaugh, Jerry, and I looked at each other.

He examined the wallet and began removing its contents. The ship was rocking in deep rolls back and forth. "Ah yes," he said, reading the writing on the back of the picture. He began studying it closely. Resting his arms on the desk he stared at it for a long time. It got very quiet. The ship was rocking over and back in traditional Langemak fashion. He sat motionless, staring, seemingly frozen in place. He swallowed. His face was moist, pallid. We looked at each other again and waited. You could almost predict what was going to happen—and suddenly it did. With no warning he vomited, turning his head aside to avoid the wallet but not completely successful. Jumping up, he ran from the wardroom and groped up the ladder, leaving us without a word, the messed-up wallet and its contents still on the desk. We got them onto a piece of cardboard and went topside. He was standing at the rail supporting himself. He mumbled something about "just recovering from dengue fever." We escorted him to the launch, handed the cardboard mess to the coxswain and waved goodbye as it pulled away. We never saw him again, nor did we ever learn anything about the wallet or the valuable information it may have contained.

Week after week of patrolling and slow-escort duty with little or no liberty began taking its toll on morale on the 648. Red Alerts and an occasional foray of enemy planes necessitating a call to General Quarters was one form of "relief," the planes more often than not flying well out of range. They provided an outlet for our desire to avenge Pearl Harbor, but the planes usually came and went quickly. We occasionally fired at them but more often than not simply watched them as they disappeared out of range. A false sense of security kept our nerves in check because we had the idea subchasers were too small for the enemy to bother with. We felt they would pick larger targets like destroyers and transports. It was largely wishful thinking however, considering the fact that sister subchasers like the 699, 743, and 742 had suffered deadly, vicious attacks. The men on those vessels didn't talk much about it, the only sign of their deadly encounters being small Japanese Rising Sun flags painted on their flying bridge rail canvas, one for each plane shot down.

As officers, we were constantly trying to find ways to relieve the monotony and keep morale as high as possible for the men. Occasionally some kind of high-jinks would break out spontaneously. Once a group of us were standing on the quarterdeck talking about nothing in particular. Someone mentioned "Wally," our former pet wallaby, and someone else recalled "Cocky" the cockatoo and soon there was a discussion of which kind of ship's pet was better. Jerry Lively, in one of his few times completely out of character, started bending and flapping his arms, making "Aaaaawks!" and strutting about like a cockatoo. I got into the act by holding my forearms up, making a dumb face and hopping about like a wallaby. But the star attraction was Captain Spaugh himself, who ran up the ladder to the flying bridge, then up the mast past the crow's nest. Grabbing the yardarm he hung by one hand, drew up his legs and scratched his ribs, making monkey hoot sounds and looking wild. The men fell all over themselves in laughter.

It was a short, spontaneous act, one of those vignettes that become stamped in one's memory.

Playing cards and acey-deucy were popular pastimes, the latter a form of backgammon. Once we ran a team tournament for crew members who played "500," a form of euchre with two pairs of players as in bridge. Jerry and I were eliminated after three rounds. The winners were Beanblossom and Beebe, who received free cartons of cigarettes and candy from the ship's store as their reward.

Relaxation on the bow. From left, clockwise: Beebe, Beanblossom, Esser, Newman

Another recreation was boxing. J. Green had been an amateur boxer, He and several others went at it now and then, a good way to let off steam. When I visited Jay a few years ago he told me how he "stiffed Cap'n Spaugh" during one of those boxing matches.

The open hatch (square, black area) leads to crew's quarters and galley

A sense of humor kept things on an even keel. Swett's sly, spontaneous clowning made life more tolerable. Once when he had the lookout watch on the flying bridge, I was the O.D. and, in the middle of the watch, went up to have a look-see. Swett was sitting in the captain's chair pretending to be buried in a book and paying no attention to anything around him. He glanced at me with a roguish look, quickly scanned the horizon and said, "There's no ships out there, sir" and buried himself in the book again. Another time when he had lookout duty in the crow's nest, I came up to the flying bridge and looked around the horizon through my binoculars. While I was doing this Swett made snoring sounds from the crow's nest, giving us both a chuckle. One time he spent a couple of hours fiddling around in his bunk with needle and thread. When he came topside he was dressed in a zoot suit. This caused a few howls of laughter around the ship. Another time we three officers were having mess in the after compartment and it was Swett's turn at mess cook duty. We officers were half-heartedly nibbling at one of Fagan's grimmer fares of Aussie frankfurters (which everyone hated), canned string beans, and cold rice. Swett emerged from the galley with the knife sharpener.

"Gentlemen," he said, "If that steak is a little tough, try this."

Almost every morning Jerry and I censored the crew's outgoing mail, a job we hated, but which was necessary because nothing could be left to chance in wartime. We looked primarily for anything that would disclose our location or operation. (Everyone wanted to tell their loved ones where they were.) One morning there was a letter addressed to "The Censor, USS SC 648" which read as follows:

I hereby dedicate the following poem to you:

The Censor

A rugged and silent man is he
Who censors the mail from off the sea.
He scans every letter, just his trusty scissors and he,
With grim pleasure and foul delight,
His eagle eye devours each word aright.
The pages seem to wither under the horrible stare.
The best of the tale is not left there.
With a little snip now and then,
Oh hell, I'll start over again.

By A. Poetic.

Swett readily admitted being the culprit. When I told him his spelling was atrocious he pretended to look blank, then, face lighting up, he said, "Oh, I spell good, huh?"

Another crew member who livened thing up was Francis Stengele, EM/2c, a kid from the Bronx who came from a poor family, had to work at an early age, and never finished high school. Short and muscular, he weighed only 130 pounds. Despite his lack of education, Stengele was smart and versatile He was useful in many ship activities, including gun maintenance, cooking when Fagan was seasick, and standing watches in the engine room. He loved to fish and every chance he got when we were in port he'd drop a line over the side. Stengele was in love with a girl named Ronnie back in the Bronx and his letters were quite passionate. Once when I was censoring his letter to Ronnie he put several X marks at the bottom for kisses and wrote: "Please don't censor the kisses Mr. Treadwell." I couldn't resist adding under it, "Ok, Stengele" and put it through. Several weeks later Stengele got a letter from Ronnie in which she wrote, "what a swell guy Mr. Treadwell must be for doing such a thing." Stengele wrote another letter with a lot of X marks at the end and I added an X mark and wrote "from Mr. Treadwell" on it. Her letter in response to that talked about nothing but the kiss I had sent her and she sent one to me in return. Stengele showed me the letter and we both agreed things had gone far enough.

Stengele's favorite epithet when he got into an argument with someone was "batshit!" He used the word so frequently it became synonymous with "Stengele." Sometimes you'd hear someone sing out "Hey, Batshit, come over here." Stengele sang a lot and was familiar with just about every tune or song ever created. He had an abundance of one-liners, short poems, or quotations. One went:

> TB or not TB,
> That is the congestion.
> Consumption be done about it?
> Of cough, of cough!

Stengele would get into arguments about things that had little to do with anything. These were usually instigated by Vernor Rice, our signalman, who owned a copy of the World Almanac. He'd look up something obscure like which state had more people, Rhode Island or Montana, and then find one or two others to act as shills to bait Stengele. A discussion would ensue, the original topic would be forgotten, and you'd hear the word "batshit" more than once.

Sometimes when we were tied up alongside a dock we'd find an open space and organize a softball game with the crewmen of a sister subchaser. Once a game was played between officers and enlisted men and, naturally, the enlisted men won by a healthy margin. I acted as umpire in a few games, enduring some uncomplimentary remarks for questionable calls during the temporary hiatus from rank or station.

Stengele working on K-gun

One shore excursion was memorable because it had a South Seas flavor we never expected. We were cruising solo along the New Guinea coast and spotted a native village in the middle of a grove of coconut palms and mangroves. Through our binoculars we could see natives on the beach launching their outrigger canoes. Spaugh decided to drop anchor. Two of the canoes approached and, with friendly gestures, we motioned for them to come alongside. The oldest man in the two canoes was the spokesman and could speak broken English. He told us his name was Augustin and a feast was taking place in the village in honor of some native laborers who were going to leave the village to work with the American soldiers. He invited us to come to their feast.

We gave Augustin some cigarettes, pipe tobacco, and candy and told him we would be over. Using our rubber raft rigged with an outboard motor, about thirteen of us paddled into the beach. The natives stood at the water's edge to greet us, a bit shyly at first, but so interested in the "long motor canoe" they became quite friendly, staring at us open-eyed and smiling, from old, skinny men with wrinkled skin, sticks and rings through their noses, and tattoo marks on their bodies, to young women naked to the waist and grass-skirted, also tattooed and with widened holes in their ear lobes.

We walked into the village carrying the only barter we had thought to bring, a case of army C-rations and forty cans of bully beef. As we approached the center of the village a man who appeared to be their chief greeted us. He was dressed in a red skirt and a cotton T-shirt. He couldn't speak English so Augustin acted as interpreter and told us the chief wanted us to feel welcome. There was a slight pause in which no one seemed to know what to say. The chief broke the silence by giving orders to a couple of boys standing by who ran over to the nearest coconut palms and began climbing. They quickly reached the coconuts and tossed several of them down. A woman picked them up and handed them to us. Esser, radioman, said he could do that and went over to one of the trees and tried climbing it barefooted, the way the boys had done. The natives giggled and laughed as he struggled, getting only a few feet before giving up.

The natives forgot their bashfulness as we began handing out cans of C-rations and bully beef. For every can we handed out a native would give something in return. Before long, trading began in earnest. The assemblage broke up into smaller groups with our men gesturing and talking with the natives, both trying to make themselves understood. Sometimes a group would shout "Augustin, Augustin!" and

Augustin would go over and settle a question for each of the bargaining parties.

Spaugh sent a couple of men back to the ship to get more cigarettes, tobacco, and candy and any other trinkets the men could find. When they returned the trading got more intense. Grass skirts, bracelets, native combs, headdresses, shells, and eating implements were the natives' offerings. The chief spoke to several natives and they ran to their huts, returning with fresh bananas, papaws, limes, squash, and coconuts. They set these on the ground in front of the chief. He motioned for Spaugh to come forward, and with Augustin's help he told us these were gifts for us. Spaugh, in the role of a modern day Captain James Cook, accepted these graciously and had us place several cigarette cartons and tins of tobacco on the ground as our offering to them. Everyone smiled and cheered.

The sailors stared unabashedly at the bare-breasted native women but they conducted themselves admirably, making no untoward advances. Our arrival had come just as their feast was about to begin but by the time the bartering and exchange of gifts had ended it was time to return to the ship. The natives accompanied us to the shoreline and there was much laughter and kidding when Swett couldn't get the outboard motor started. The chief said something; Augustin told us it meant "After the war you come by to stay."

Life on a subchaser in the Pacific at times could be droll. We were cruising independently at 11 knots one fine day; the sky was clear, the seas calm. I had the watch and was on the flying bridge. In the crow's nest was Beck, our yeoman, searching the horizon with his binoculars.

"Sir, there's an object broad on the starboard bow. It looks about four or five thousand yards out," he sang out in his clear, distinctive voice.

Looking through my navy-issue 7x50 binoculars, I could see, sure enough, something was on the horizon, bobbing up and down.

"It looks like a raft," Beck reported.

I gave orders in the voice tube to change course to bring the object dead ahead. Beck was transfixed, his binoculars pressed to his eyes. As we drew closer and slowed he began a series of short reports, each a few seconds apart.

"Yessir, it looks like a raft all right ..."

"It looks as though it has a sail ..."

"It looks like something on the raft, sir ..."

"Sir, it looks like a body! ..."

"Yessir, it is a body! ..."

"And it's not moving, either ..."

Beebe and I couldn't make it out. For the life of us we couldn't see anything resembling a body—or a raft, for that matter.

"Sir, do you get a smell of a dead body?" Beck asked.

"No," I replied.

"Well, I do, sir," Beck said. He raised his voice in excitement. "That raft has a dead body on it, sir."

When we got close enough we made out the details. It was no raft and there was no dead body. It appeared to be an empty oil drum with a wooden post lashed to it. It had all the appearance of a jury-rigged sea buoy broken loose from its moorings. A few rounds from one of the 20 mm guns sank it to prevent it from being a navigational hazard and that was that. But George Green made sure everyone knew about "the raft and the dead body lashed to it" and Beck was kidded unmercifully about it ever after.

Victor Beck, a native of Philadelphia who had been in the wallpaper business with his father when the war broke out, was one of our plank owners, a capable and trustworthy yeoman. The yeoman on a ship handles payroll, personnel transfer papers, supply records, official correspondence, and all the other paperwork necessary to transact a ship's business. On the 648 Beck was also in charge of the petty cash box and ship's store. His "office" was a desk and file cabinet squeezed between the radio shack on the port side and the sonar room on the starboard side, just forward of the wardroom. An Underwood typewriter sat on the desk over which hung a cabinet with doors that locked—the ship's store—containing cigarettes, pipe tobacco, candy, and a few toiletry supplies. The file cabinet held all the ship's papers, correspondence files, and spare office supplies. Under the desk was the ship's safe, containing classified material, including the codebooks.

Like most of the men, Beck wore several hats depending upon the job at hand. He was a very good helmsman and an excellent lookout (dead body excepted) and his battle station was as loader on the 40 mm gun. He had an indefinable quality, the set of the jaw, the well-chiseled features, the clear blue eyes. It indicated character and class. He always looked directly at you when talking and his voice was clear and well modulated with an inflection and a use of words that would have made Tom Brokaw envious. His knowledge of navy forms, procedures, and protocol was gargantuan, at least so I believed, probably because of my own ignorance of such things. He spent much time studying new directives, manuals, and procedures, honing his skills as a yeoman. Many times I remember returning late from a ship's movie or poker game and passing him at his desk, hunched over the typewriter, working on a report or unfinished correspondence.

Beck was popular with the crew. He talked on many subjects, articulately and with enthusiasm. He kept up with politics, sports, and business and participated in the many discussions and arguments about these things among his shipmates. He was very proud of his kid brother who was in the Air Force back in the States training to be a bomber. With great pride he once showed me a sheepskin-lined leather jacket he had bought in Brisbane for his kid brother. But the crew would ride him because he talked so much about his brother, his admiration and affection unabashed and genuine. With the arrival of every new mail he'd announce the latest news about his kid brother. When he announced that his brother had made 2d lieutenant and gotten his wings the crew kidded him.

"Now you'll have to salute him, Beck."

"You better shape up or he'll bust you."

Beck didn't mind. "Well, he's flying a B-25 now, he expects to go overseas pretty soon. Maybe he'll come out here."

Someone: "Jesus Christ, one Beck is already one too many out here."

"Hey," Beck would say, "He could take on any two of you with his hands tied behind his back."

Someone: "Aaah, those flyboys have the best duty of anyone in the service. They get waited on hand and foot. They'll spoil him. You'll never know him when he comes home. He won't even look at you, Beck."

"Oh, yeah? That'll be the day!" Beck said, "The day my own kid brother won't look at me? You guys are just jealous."

Beck was the ship's storekeeper. He watched over the inventory, balanced his ledgers, and posted notices about price changes, PX hours, etc. The men accused him of raising prices and pocketing the extra profit, referring to him as "Herman the vermin" or "Jake the snake," all of which Beck took good-naturedly. George Green, who usually referred to him as "that miserable critter the yeoman," nicknamed him "Granny" after the floating dead man incident

Cigarettes were the most popular item in ship's store, with Camel, Lucky Strike, Chesterfield and Kool the chief brands. Around this time Pall Mall introduced a new kind of cigarette that had a filter. The store did a lively trade in stationery, candy, Dr. Lyons tooth powder, and fountain pen ink (ballpoint pens were a postwar innovation).

There was a time when we went almost three weeks without mail and everyone was complaining. Mail from home was probably the single most desirable morale builder and when this lapsed, morale usually sank to new lows. So it was with special delight that our mail detail finally brought back four big sacks of mail for the men on the 648. As ever, Spaugh enjoyed doling out the many letters, magazines, newspapers, and packages. After that the ship quieted down, each man absorbed in reading the latest news from families and loved ones with an occasional remark like "Wow! She said her first word—'Daddy'!" or "Jeez, my dad broke his leg falling off a ladder."

Several minutes passed before someone noticed Beck sitting on an ammo locker, letter in hand, slumped forward. His head was down and his shoulders shook. He had just learned his kid brother had been killed in Texas in a training flight. The news passed from man to man with a series of silent nods and nudges. A painful silence settled over the 648, a silence that lasted several days. Even the captain, normally thick-skinned, was visibly touched as he talked quietly with Beck. Everyone felt helpless, unable to relieve his pain. Beck took it very hard. For a long time he kept to himself, talking very little and only when necessary. He faithfully continued his duties, stood his watches, and worked harder than ever, but his enthusiasm and spirit were missing. As time went by he became more like his old self, smiling and joking, but he never mentioned his kid brother again.

In October of that year Beck finally got his orders to return to the States. He had served two years and three months on the 648, one of the longest tours of anyone who served before or after on the ship. He was next to the last of the plank owners to leave, and the ship would never be quite the same without him.

At the time he left, I was skipper of the 648 and I knew I would miss him badly. I stood with him at the gangway as we waited for a motor launch to pick him up to take him on the first leg of his trip homeward. The gulf that separated enlisted men from officers was still there, but Beck was more than just another member of the crew. We had done many things together and we had high respect for each other. We made small talk to cover our real feelings. I thanked him for his work as a yeoman and told him he would be missed. The launch pulled alongside and the two of us shook hands. He bent down to pick up his duffle bag and jacket. Tossing the duffle bag into the launch, he climbed down the ladder, clutching the jacket tightly. It was the jacket he had bought eighteen months before, in Brisbane, for his kid brother. The launch, with Beck in the stern, moved swiftly away.

After the war Beck ran his father's wallpaper business in Philadelphia, and when he retired he and his wife Eve moved to Florida. I had dinner with them in the late '60s when I was in Miami on business; we exchanged Christmas cards several years after that. Attempts to locate him in recent years have failed.

On February 1, 1944, I left the ship and flew to Sydney, Australia, for ten days of leave. Three days later Spaugh and twelve crew members also left for Sydney. Jerry Lively took temporary command and for most of the time we were gone the ship lay at anchor in Milne Bay.

My recollections of Sydney are summed up in a letter home:

> Today I drank a quart of cold fresh milk accompanied by a generous piece of Boston cream pie with ice cream. This was served to me in a real restaurant by a pretty blonde waitress who smiled at me. Last night I slept between two fresh white sheets on a comfortable bed in my own room. The only noises I remember before falling asleep were a dog barking, someone's heels clicking on the pavement, a fellow fixing a flat tire and cursing. This morning when I awoke I heard birds singing, the same dog barking and children's voices in the street.

The U.S.O. had a place in Sydney where men in uniform could go for relaxation. There was dancing to live music almost every night and it was there that I met an Australian girl named Diana Walker who, a day or two later, invited me to dinner at her family's house. Her father was a prominent businessman and their house was a large, well-appointed stone mansion. The family pet was a black Labrador and Diana liked classical music, so it was good just to play with the dog, sit around listening to music and making ordinary talk with no reminder of the war. Diana and I never got very romantic, but after I returned to the ship, I received two or three long letters from her (a little too long) that looked as though she was leaning that way. The correspondence between us petered out.

As I mentioned, Spaugh and several enlisted men were also in Sydney. We spent our leaves separately, probably because we not only wanted to get away from the ship but also from each other. We all returned together, however, on

DD 527, the *Ammen*. The voyage from Sydney to Milne Bay took no time at all but it gave me a brief idea of life aboard a destroyer. Compared with a subchaser, she was a luxury ship. At officers' mess, for instance, we had white linen tablecloths and napkins, great food with big bowls of ice cream for dessert. There were movies at night, a laundry, an air-conditioned radio shack—and I didn't see a single cockroach.

Typical convoy scene viewed from flying bridge. Squall approaches in background

On February 27 we were all safely back aboard the 648, nested with several other subchasers alongside the USS Fulton. Little had happened in our absence; the ship had been idle and most of the rust had been scraped and painted over. That night, after sunset, several officers and crew members were lounging around the quarterdeck, smoking, talking, or just sitting. An amplifier blared out Kay Kyser's music with lots of Bing Crosby and Frank Sinatra. Junior Fairlie, our "motormac," was sitting next to me. He leaned back, his hands clasped behind his head. "Gawddamn," he drawled in his country Texas accent, "this sure is heaven. What more could a man ask for than a good comfortable chair, a cool breeze, and the radio playing good music? Gawddamn!" Of course, everyone who knew Fairlie knew he was talking tongue-in-cheek, thinking of only two things: liquor and women.

New Guinea 131

Rope work on the dock at Buna New Guinea. Aussie soldiers look on.

Sister subchaser SC 749 coming alongside

Salt water bath

Salt sun bath

Salt water swim

Fetching salt water

New Guinea   133

Hosing ship's bottom to remove barnacles

Writing letters home in the after crew's compartment

134   Taste of Salt

Painting never ends   Beebe, QM2C at signal lamp

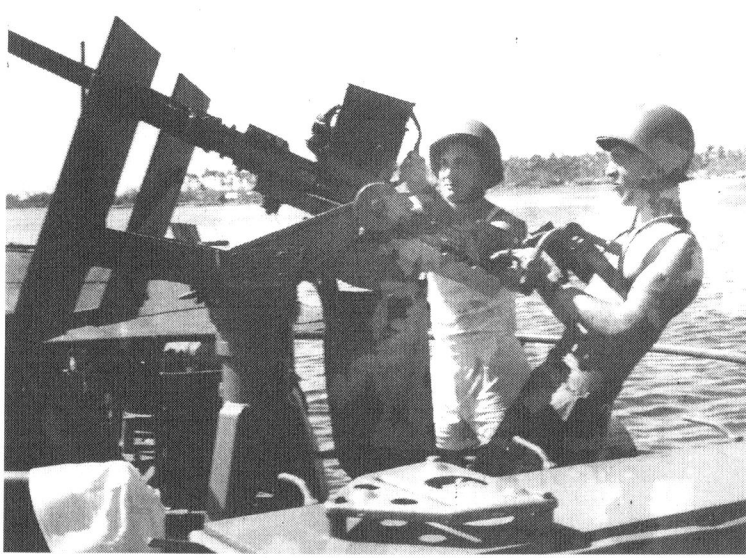

Keltner and Esser man the aft 20mm AA gun

New Guinea 135

Native boy climbs for coconuts

Esser attempts without success

McFall, F2C and Beck Y2C with New Guinea natives

The author with natives

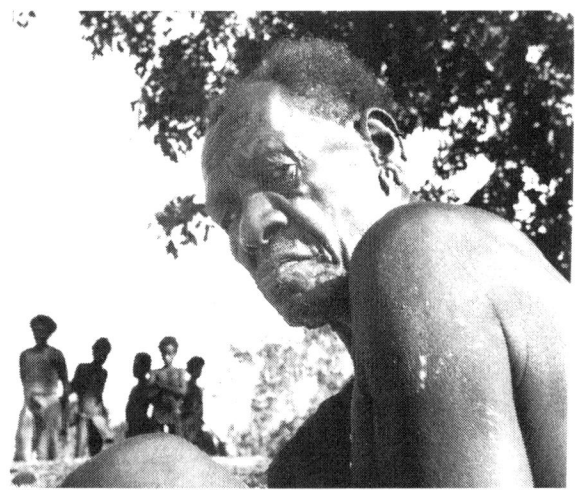

New Guinea senior citizen

Aitape

On April 12, 1944, Ensign Glenn F. Welsh reported for duty as third officer and I was promoted to executive officer. Jerry received orders to take command of SC 748 and left the 648 a day or two later. I was sorry to see him go. He had been my good teacher and mentor. He hated the ship and he hated Spaugh, but he was an excellent officer who served well and kept his mouth shut. His leaving coincided with a new era on SC 648. The endless series of dull escort trips and harbor patrols was finally to be interrupted.

We were selected to be the inner control vessel for a landing at Aitape, one of the three beachhead landing points for the Hollandia invasion, a major thrust in General MacArthur's drive to the Philippines. Most of us welcomed the thought of a relief from the long monotony of patrols and escort voyages. Our enthusiasm leaped even more when we learned we were to be the flagship for the landing control officer, a four-striper navy captain.

No one on SC 648 had ever heard of Captain John W. Jamison, nor did we have any inkling of his meritorious background and experience. All we knew was that he was to be the landing control officer at Aitape and would be using our ship as his flagship. That alone was enough to make us work hard to tidy up and get things ready to have him aboard.

Preparations began immediately. Everyone turned to in an effort to spruce things up and make them look more shipshape. We wanted the 648 to look like a navy warship instead of like, well, the dirty, cramped, cockroach-ridden spitkit she really was. We decided to holystone the main deck, something we had never done before. Although it was a backbreaking job and there were a few grumbles, it did whiten the deck and improve appearances topside. Junior Fairlie, his engines now in pretty good shape, decided to spruce things up in the engine room. He assigned "Red" Westring, a young seaman striking for an engine room rating, the job of painting all brightwork in the engine room with aluminum paint. Gunner's mates Jay Green and Lou George began work on all the ordnance, beginning with the mousetraps and depth charges, carefully and methodically stripping, cleaning, and greasing all the gun mechanisms.

Fagan took two men over to the *U.S.S.Fulton* and brought back cases, bags, and crates of food a level better than the Spam, dehydrated potatoes, canned chili, canned beans, and powdered milk we had been eating most of the time. We now had a good supply of fresh eggs, sides of beef and Australian mutton, new potatoes, Jello, and other delicacies, including a bonus of several gallons of vanilla ice cream.

By now I was considerably more experienced. I felt quite at home on the 648 and, along with everyone else on 648, was keyed up for Aitape and the presence on board of a real navy captain. Morale was never higher as the day for the landing approached.

On April 17 we were anchored in Langemak when we received orders to send a boat to pick up the captain from an LCT a half-mile away. Our only boat was our little wherry without a motor. Spaugh dispatched four men with paddles to fetch the captain in the wherry. Two men would have been enough but Spaugh felt four paddles would get the errand done more quickly. When they returned with Captain Jamison an hour later it made quite a picture, with the captain sitting in the stern in full regalia, wearing his battle helmet, fatigues, and a Colt .45 automatic pistol at his hip. The weight of five men in the wherry caused it to ride precariously low in the water.

I mentioned earlier the long swells in the harbor at Langemak, and as usual we were rolling in typical Langemak fashion. Just as the wherry came alongside, a swell rolled in, causing the wherry to smack hard against the side of the ship, despite efforts to fend it off. Captain Jamison, gripping the gunwales in the stern, didn't look very pleased. There being no ladder or gangway, we extended hands and managed to get him aboard without incident, though we were a bit lubberly about it and it was a poor introduction for him.

Although Captain Jamison was only 42, our first impression was that he looked terribly old. He had a medium build, with a hint of a paunch about his midsection. His hair and mustache and eyebrows were slightly reddish, his complexion ruddy, and he had blue eyes that could look through you. He was neither pleasant nor unpleasant, his whole demeanor being that of someone who had a job to do, whose stay aboard our ship was unfortunate but would be 100 percent business.

Ens. Glenn F. Welsh, our new Third Officer

After introductions Spaugh led him into the pilothouse, inviting him for a tour of the ship, which he declined. Instead, he asked for coffee and began unpacking things from his duffle bag, including an air mattress. He solved a dilemma for us by announcing he would sleep in the chartroom. We had pondered the sleeping problem beforehand, and since Spaugh and I were old navy hands by now, had decided to do things the navy way. The lowest-ranking officer would have to give up his bunk in the wardroom and fend for himself. Ensign Welsh would have paid the price with his bunk but was saved by the captain.

We watched, fascinated, as Captain Jamison showed us how the air mattress inflated with an ingenious built-in pump. This over, the ship returned to its routine and began preparing to get under way. Spaugh took his station on the flying bridge and sang out the orders:

"Light off the main engines! Weigh anchor! Set Condition 1!"

Five minutes later we were under way on various courses and speeds departing Cape Cretin anchorage to rendezvous with Task Unit 76.6 outside the harbor. Our destination for the first leg of the trip was Seeadler Harbor, Manus Island, in the Admiralties, the staging area where the main force would gather for the final run to the beaches of Hollandia, Aitape, and Tanahmerah Bay.

As we were steaming out from Finschhafen to join the other ships, our old friend SC 981 was running parallel to our starboard side. Both ships were doing 13 knots—a pretty good speed for SCs. As if by mutual consent, the two subchasers began converging, gradually coming closer together as they steamed along. Spaugh and "Denny" Cutler, the skipper of the 981, were good friends, and several crew members on each SC knew each other, so Spaugh told the helmsman to maneuver us even closer. Soon both vessels were steaming along side by side at 13 knots, only fifty feet apart, bow wakes colliding in an even pattern of white froth. Spaugh was laughing and calling over to the other skipper, and the men on both subchasers were lined along the rails yelling and waving to each other.

I was standing on the quarterdeck just aft of the pilothouse, enjoying the commotion when Captain Jamison emerged from the charthouse and looked across at the other subchaser.

"Treadwell, what's going on here?" he asked, querulously.

"Um, well, the captain, uh, we know that ship pretty well, and I guess the captain wanted, you know, to say something to the skipper," I fumbled.

For a full minute Captain Jamison looked across the churning waters, his hands on hips, the two subchasers racing neck and neck out of the harbor, the men calling across the waves to each other in good-natured banter and cheers.

The captain turned, his expression that of complete distaste. He shook his head, unbelieving.

"This is no subchaser," he said flatly, in a tone everyone could hear. "This is a goddamned yacht!" He returned into the pilothouse.

The men who heard him doubled over laughing and I had all I could do to stifle my own. Captain Jamison had stamped his appraisal in words that became immortal on our ship. From that moment whenever something went wrong around the ship, we had the perfect excuse: "For criminy sakes, you dumb jackass, what did you expect? You're not on a subchaser, you're on a goddammed yacht."

Another time, Captain Jamison emerged from the chartroom just as George Green, one of our sloppiest dressers, was passing by on his way to the after crew quarters. On this occasion he wore ragged cutoffs dragged low by the weight of a long knife, fashioned from an old file, that he always carried in a sheath hanging from his belt on his scrawny backside. He called it his "frogsticker," and it was his trademark. A dirty skivvy shirt hung out of his pants, flapping at the waist. I observed the captain studying Green disapprovingly as he disappeared down the after compartment hatch and made a mental note to myself to speak to Green. Nodding toward him, Jamison said to me, "Is that an example of your dress code?"

I'm not sure what I said, but I do recall wondering why I seemed to be the only officer present when Jamison disapproved of something.

Our convoy to Seeadler Harbor was in company with the destroyer Stockton, SOPA, and several old faithful workhorse SCs who had been with us for many months, including the 637, 742, 703, 743, and 981, all providing a screen for a group of eighteen LCTs. The trip took thirty hours and was uneventful, with no breakdowns and no enemy sub or plane contacts. By 7:15 p.m. on April 18 we had dropped anchor in Seeadler Harbor and were safely nestled among an armada of 215 vessels that had converged on Seeadler as the staging area for the invasion.

The Hollandia invasion was to be the largest yet for MacArthur's Navy in the Southwest Pacific. Three separate points on the coast of New Guinea were selected for landing, the Western Attack Group at Tanahmera Bay, the Central Attack Group at Humboldt Bay, Hollandia, and the Eastern Attack Group at Aitape. Seeadler Harbor at Manus, in the Admiralty Islands, was the rendezvous point for all ships participating.

C.A.Westring F3C

We spent the next day at Manus refueling and taking on water, making last-minute preparations. A moment of diversion came in mid-morning when we were taking on fuel and water. I was again standing at my favorite spot on the quarterdeck, and Captain Jamison stood beside me, observing. Chief Junior Fairlie, in charge of the engine room, came over and showed me the end of one finger, which he held out for me to inspect. The finger had a dab of aluminum paint on it. "Yes, so?" I asked. In those days aluminum paint came in two containers, the contents of which had to be thoroughly mixed. One can held the aluminum powder and the other a lacquer that smelled like banana oil. He said, "Look at this." He wiped it clean with one swipe of a rag. "The kid painted down there four days ago. It looked great. Just now I wiped my finger along it to make sure it was dry. Everything's as wet as the day he painted it." The "kid" he referred to was "Red" Westring, a youngster who tried very hard but somehow managed to foul up the simplest task.

Just then Westring emerged up the ladder from the after crew quarters. The chief beckoned him over. "Hey, Westring, what did you mix with that aluminum powder?"

"Uh, I used diesel oil," Westring said.

"You used what?" The three of us stared at him unbelievingly. He winced.

"Oooh, gee," he faltered, "I knew I should have used lube oil."

Captain Jamison looked at me, rolled his eyes, and walked away. Now it was his turn to laugh. Fairlie took the hapless Westring aside and quietly told him, "Get the hell below and clean it up."

At 4:23 p.m. on the 19th we were under way in company with eighteen LCIs, five SCs, and two YMS minesweepers, crossing the Bismarck Sea to the shores of New Guinea. We cruised at different speeds and changed courses frequently to throw off any clues the enemy might pick up from our movements. All night and the following day and night we steamed in this fashion. At 5:45 on the evening of the 21st, Task Group TG3 broke away from the others and set course for Aitape. The four SCs in this group were the 648, 637, 742, and 981. The 703, 738, and 743 remained on course with the Central Group for the landing at Humboldt Bay.

The beauty of the evening before the landing was lost to most of us because of the tension building up over the coming invasion. The wind subsided and the seas flattened. The Southern Cross hung overhead like four bright jewels. We could have imagined ourselves tourists on a South Seas cruise, marveling at such natural splendor. Midnight passed into the wee hours of the morning, and the sea became even smoother until, with the first faint tinges of dawn, the water was glass-slick. At 5:00 a.m. we saw the land, a low, flat, grey smudge on the horizon, slightly out of focus from the faint mist rising from the sea.

Some moments etch themselves deeply within the subconscious. Minute details—the smell, the quiet, the gray, the damp, the chill—stay with you forever. H-hour at Aitape was just such a moment for me; years later I was moved to recall it in these words:

> Close your eyes, old man, Listen.
> Hear the hiss of bow through slicksmooth water.
> Smell the swamp mist, smell the damp rot,
> Smell the stale sweat of 3,000 sons at dawn,
> Off the beach at Aitape.
>
> Tremble in the chill air, old man.
> Shove dryspit down your throat.
> Suck in the roar. Listen.
> Hear the death raining down
> On the beach at Aitape.
>
> Open your eyes old man. Look.
> See the butchery where once
> Was the beach at Aitape.

At a point 8,000 yards from Blue Beach we slowed, moving quietly into the Aitape roadsteads that lay between small islands on both sides. The beach, 1,200 yards wide, was dead ahead. On the flying bridge Captain Jamison studied the approach through his binoculars, and Spaugh leaned into the voice tube, quietly giving orders to the helm. The ticklish business of positioning the 648 correctly in the poorly charted waters had begun. Rice, signalman/1c, stood on the bow taking soundings, and Beebe, quartermaster, took azimuth bearings in rapid succession, reporting each change in position. The 648 responded easily, as though she herself knew what to do. "Right rudder slowly" ... "Ease the rudder" ... "Port engine stop" ... "All engines stop" ... "All engines back one-third" ... "Left rudder slowly" ... "Ready anchor detail" ... "All engines stop" ... "Let go the anchor."

We were anchored 1,500 yards from Blue Beach. The dim light of dawn was just beginning to show faintly on the eastern horizon. SC 637, outer control vessel, dropped her anchor 3,000 yards out. Captain Jamison was satisfied. It was 06:23 a.m. Further out, nine APDs—one for each wave—carried the assault teams and their landing craft. They began launching the boats and slung over their sides the cargo nets that the troops used for scrambling down into the boats. SCs 981 and 742 stood in, ready to fire rockets when ordered. Two AK cargo ships, the USS *Etamin* and USS *Bootes*, made their way slowly down Aitape roads. Farther out, seven destroyers trained their 5-inch guns at Blue Beach, and the cruisers *Phoenix, Nashville*, and *Boise* brought their 8-inch guns to bear. Somewhere out of sight and over the horizon were the escort carriers *Sangamon, Suwanee, Chenango,* and *Santee*.

At 6:30 we felt a whooooossh overhead, so close we pulled in our shoulders and ducked at first, but later got used to it. This was followed by a deep booooooom! Then another whoosh, with a second boooooom! Then a third, and then they kept coming in, one after the other. The beach began erupting in a huge cloud of black smoke that quickly rose and spread out, covering the sky. The booms and explosions melded into a cacophony of sound, bouncing off the land mass and filling the atmosphere with an odd, supernatural noise, as though you were in a giant echo chamber of drums being pounded by the gods themselves. The roar, mixed with the gloom of dawn and the smoke, resembled something you'd feel all around you while approaching Dante's inferno. It was more overwhelming and more powerful than anything we on the 648 had ever experienced. It lasted twenty minutes, after which the guns suddenly stopped and dive-bombers from the carriers came swooping in to bomb and strafe the beach for ten more minutes. From our ship we saw quite a show—a scene of complete, total destruction.

The first wave of landing boats with the men from 163rd Regimental Combat approached and circled our ship. Captain Jamison went aft to the stern and held the starter's flag high. It was the black-and-white navy Negat flag, his own, not that from our flag bag. The men in the landing boats looked young and tough, their faces smeared with blacking, one smoking a cigar, another waving a small American flag, a few laughing and waving, others just staring. Jamison checked his watch, then brought the flag down sharply. With a loud roar, the boats sprang ahead at full speed toward the beach.

D-Day at Aitape A;ril 20, 1944

A second group of boats approached and began circling the 648. Again Captain Jamison checked his watch and brought down the flag. SCs 981 and 742 let go with their rockets, raking Blue Beach for a final time just before the first wave of landing boats arrived. Jamison waved in nine groups until all were gone. From first to last wave took only ten minutes.

With the last wave of boats gone and no more bombardment there was a strange stillness, the only sounds the soft hum of the generators and the low rumble of our diesels. Through binoculars we watched the boats as they went into the beach. One boat broached in the moderate surf and another was swamped, but most of the boats beached and disembarked the troops in good fashion. With the beach secured, the LSTs and LCTs wasted no time coming in to discharge their cargoes. A dozen or so of these ungainly but technically correct craft beached themselves, opened their bow gates, and unloaded tanks, artillery weapons, Caterpillar tractors, communication equipment, and other gear. The entire landing went smoothly and was impressive for its show of power and efficiency.

The *Etamin* passed by close aboard on its way toward the beach. As part of the second wave, she carried a thousand additional combat troops to support the first waves of troops already ashore. In her forward hold were six thousand tons of ammunition, land mines, detonators, and boxed TNT. Her after holds were crammed with drums containing several thousand gallons of high-octane aircraft gasoline, a virtual floating bomb. Minutes before, the *Etamin* assisted in the bombardment of Tumleo Island. Had the enemy returned fire from two pillboxes on Tumleo, a direct hit on the Etamin could have blown her out of the water. The *Etamin* was one of the few ships in the Seventh Fleet manned by an all-Coast Guard crew.

We weighed anchor and Spaugh maneuvered us alongside the *Etamin* to permit Captain Jamison to board her.

As senior officer present, Captain Jamison was now the beachmaster and the temporary port director at Aitape. His responsibility was to coordinate ship-to-shore activities and make sure the unloading proceeded smoothly and efficiently. The *Etamin* moved in slowly and dropped her anchor about 400 yards offshore, lowering her crane booms fore and aft to begin the task of unloading her cargo. Besides the ammunition and gasoline, the cargo included sections of landing track for the Tadji airstrip. Army stevedores would take over the job of unloading, and a Works Wing of the Royal Australian Air Force would make the airstrip ready for use. Several LCVs (Landing Craft, Vehicles) would assist, plying back and forth from the *Etamin* to the beach. It would be hard, sweaty, dangerous work, and it would take a week or longer to unload all her cargo.

We weighed anchor and moved farther out, where, for the remainder of the day, we slowly patrolled the roadstead. Thus, while everyone was working hard at the beach, we were able to relax somewhat—those of us not on watch, that is. There was no sign of the enemy, either on land or in the air. By sunset the LSTs and LCTs had discharged their cargoes, backed off the beach, and anchored offshore. Few warships were visible, although they remained in the vicinity, as evidenced by the constant chatter overheard in our radio shack. We picked up Captain Jamison from the *Etamin* and returned to patrol position for the night, sharing this duty with SC 637.

The following day we moved in close to Tumleo Island in company with the rocket SCs and laid down a barrage with our 40 mm and 20 mm guns, setting an enemy oil dump on fire. The fire burned several days, sending up swirls of dense black smoke that covered the sky all the time we were there.

Tumleo Island. Japanese oil dump destroyed.

The entire operation so far had gone quite smoothly, and Captain Jamison was pleased. For the first time since coming aboard, he came below and ate evening chow with us, chatting with several crew members. We learned that the beachhead had been secured with only two men killed and thirteen wounded. General MacArthur had been advised by his intelligence corps that there were 3,500 Japanese soldiers at Aitape. With the possibility of shore fire from the outlying islands, and not knowing exactly what submarine or aircraft activity the enemy would use, he wanted to be sure our forces were adequate. It turned out to be overkill, the only enemy action being some sporadic rifle fire that was quickly dispatched. The surprising lack of opposition was because the Japanese occupation force at Aitape was made up of service personnel instead of infantry soldiers. When the shelling started, they had been taken completely by surprise and fled inland, leaving their fires going and breakfasts uneaten.

The next several days at Aitape passed uneventfully. By sunset of the second day most of the escort carriers and cruisers had returned to Manus, and by April 24 all that remained at Aitape were the *Etamin*, the 648, the 637, a couple of seagoing tugs, two destroyers, and a scattered few LCIs and LCTs. During this period we spent our time patrolling in alternate shifts with the 637 and taking Captain Jamison wherever he wanted to go, usually to the *Etamin*.

By April 27, a week after the landing, we were still engaged in this activity. The unloading operation had been going smoothly, though slowly. By now the *Etamin*'s cargo was more than half unloaded. At 8:00 p.m. I took over the watch from Glenn Welsh. We were still maintaining antisubmarine patrol, cruising slowly back and forth 2,000 yards out from the *Etamin*. Moyer was at his station below, pinging away with the sonar. It began drizzling lightly, hardly enough to warrant wet weather gear.

At 9:00 p.m. Captain Jamison came up to the bridge, followed shortly by Spaugh. The three of us talked about nothing in particular, though I recall the captain talking about his days at the naval academy, answering our questions and reminiscing. By now we were more comfortable with him aboard. With things on the beach going well, he seemed more tolerant of our ship's routine and our quirky, reservist ways. He never interfered with Spaugh's command of the ship and left all operations of that nature to be performed by us, unimpeded and uncriticized, with a forbearance that we all appreciated. He stayed by himself much of the time but occasionally would relax and open up a little. That night he was in rare good humor and told us about his family, his life in the navy, the ships he had served on, places he had been, people he had known. What he didn't tell us (we learned later) was that he had distinguished himself in the November 1942 landing in North Africa, when he was planning officer and beachmaster for the Casablanca landing at Fedhala. The landing was difficult because of darkness and poor communications. Changes in beach sites and the disposition of landing craft had to be made on the spot. Commander Jamison quickly assessed the situation and boldly changed the original landing plan by diverting the boats to other beaches, despite the objections of several high-ranking army officers. The changes worked to advantage, helped greatly in securing the beachhead, and saved many lives. The ruffled feelings among army brass subsided when the smoke cleared and General George Patton publicly announced that "Red" Jamison had "saved the whole goddam operation." Shortly after this, Jamison, a no-nonsense, take-charge officer, was promoted to captain. He was then reassigned to the Pacific Theater and became amphibious training officer on Admiral Barbey's staff—his status when he came aboard the 648.

The three of us were making small talk on the bridge when we heard the faint drone of a single-engine plane, followed by the sudden appearance of a bright light overhead—so bright it was like daylight. You could read a newspaper in it. A second light followed the first and we could see the gray hull of the *Etamin* etched against the dark hills behind it, looking ghostly, like a surrealist painting.

"They're here," Jamison said, "Skipper, you'd better call general quarters."

The enemy had dropped two starshells, and we were lit up like broad daylight. Spaugh ordered Beebe to sound general quarters and have the anchor detail haul up the anchor.

"They're looking us over," Captain Jamison said. "They'll be back."

The captain looked at the *Etamin* through his binoculars. We stood, waiting. It began raining harder. Ten minutes passed. Just as I was beginning to think nothing was going to happen, we heard another droning noise. This time you could tell the plane was much lower, but still we could see nothing. Suddenly, out to seaward, one of the destroyers started firing its 40 mm guns, the white tracers streaming into the night sky. We heard a plane coming in from seaward, passing directly overhead, low, going toward the beach. We still couldn't see it. A second plane came in overhead, this one even lower, but we couldn't see that one either.

Then we heard a dull boom and saw a shower of sparks spewing up out of the *Etamin*'s stack like a fireworks fountain display.

"They got her!" shouted Captain Jamison. "They got the *Etamin!*"

Through binoculars I could see the sparks blowing up from the stack, then a billow of white and black smoke and then more sparks. We were facing her starboard side, and as I swept my glasses slowly along her hull I could just make out something black at the waterline that I hadn't seen before. The aerial torpedo had made a perfect hit just abaft the *Etamin*'s center, at the waterline.

Jamison said, "Get under way. We've got to get over there and push her into the beach before she settles."

"Left full rudder, all engines ahead full!" Spaugh ordered. I studied the *Etamin* through my binoculars. It looked as high in the water as ever. I couldn't see any activity topsides. Nobody seemed to be on the deck. Except for the big black mark on her side she looked just the same. We came about in a tight quarter turn and headed full speed for the *Etamin.*

Spaugh let out a cry of pain. He crouched over with one hand at his face, covering one eye. We were steaming full speed towards the *Etamin*, closing fast. Spaugh was in some sort of agony. "Kee-rist! Damn! Dammit! Goddamn!" he hissed.

"What's wrong, what happened, what's the matter?" I asked him.

He had bent down to pick up something and in doing so had rammed the tip of the antenna from a walkie-talkie left lying on the deck right into his eye, blinding it. He was in excruciating pain.

"God damn! Goddamn!" was all he could say, then, "Ted, make sure they get the lines ready up forward. Jesus! Is it bleeding?" [It wasn't.] I could see our men were ready with lines. We were 200 yards from the *Etamin*, closing at full speed. It was raining harder. The men on the 40 mm gun up forward looked up at the bridge in alarm. Someone shouted, "Cap'n, Cap'n!"

Jamison bellowed, "Stop the ship, goddammit, you're going to crash it!"

Paul straightened up, leaned into the voice tube. "All engines stop! Left full rudder! All engines back one third!" Luckily, Lou George at the wheel had already begun turning. The 648 slowed, yawing and rolling from its back wake. The *Etamin* loomed over us, fifty yards away.

"Back full! Right full rudder!"

Again, Lou George had already turned the wheel. We heeled over, dangerously close. The gray steel wall of the *Etamin* came at us. We braced for a collision. Things happened so fast that no one had time to move from his station (assuming no one was too scared to move). There was a violent, shuddering surge as the screws dug in, the reverse wake churning from our stern. The 648 slewed and stopped short of the gray wall by five feet, the water between the two ships heaving up and splashing the men on the 40 mm gun.

Spaugh had done it again. Ever flamboyant in his approaches and dockings, he had by accident surpassed himself, this time with only one eye.

Jamison, furious, had no time for talk. His job was to try to push the *Etamin* into the beach so as to save her cargo. He went down the ladder to our quarterdeck and yelled up to the *Etamin* to drop a ladder so that he could come aboard. It was still raining.

Clad in nothing but their skivvies, men were clustered twenty feet above us along the deck of the *Etamin*. We drifted slowly along the starboard side, the steel wall leaning high over us. She had begun settling slightly to starboard, causing her main deck to appear as though it were hanging over our heads. On her deck there was nothing but mass confusion. I saw one officer bawling out orders, with no one listening or paying attention. Men were shouting down to us.

Then we saw it: a twenty-foot-diameter gaping, hissing hole, with a mass of broken, jagged metal, thin wraiths of steam issuing from cracked pipes, and oil drums floating in the water lapping in and out of the opening. The smell of gas was everywhere. Passing slowly aft, we kept yelling for someone to take our lines. A monkey fist went up but no one grabbed it. The men on the *Etamin* were in panic. We heard someone yelling something that sounded like "Abandon ship!" Then, like a human waterfall, the trembling, half-naked men scrambled down the side of the steel wall, dropping on our deck until there were fifty or sixty of them crowded together, shivering, cold and frightened, some of them whimpering. They were everywhere on our deck, making it hard for us to handle lines. The rain continued.

We finally got lines secured and Spaugh, nosing the 648 against the *Etamin*'s side like a tugboat, gave the order to the engine room for full power. The screws thrashed and churned the water violently and the lines tautened, creaking under the strain. We herded the *Etamin*'s men out of the way, in case our lines let go. The *Etamin* was worse than a steel pier. She wouldn't budge. An LCT arrived and began pushing at her bow, but the *Etamin* was immovable.

Fifty-three years later, while researching this story, I learned that the *Etamin*'s captain had given the order to weigh anchor. A boatswain's mate went below to bleed the anchor winch lines but later reported that the lines "turned over slow and then stopped." The ship could not have weighed anchor in any event. The anchor chain had been almost completely paid out to 120 fathoms, and the ship was anchored so securely that a battleship couldn't have moved her.

While all this was going on, Captain Jamison kept hollering up for someone to lower a ladder so that he could go aboard. After much difficulty, a ladder was dropped and he climbed aboard the *Etamin* to assist her captain, George Steadman. The men from the *Etamin* thought we had come alongside to rescue them from their ship, which they thought was sinking. Fagan sent up mugs of coffee and hot soup from the galley and blankets were passed around for the shivering, frightened men still in shock, still in their skivvies. Many of them were army stevedores assigned to the ship for the unloading work. If the *Etamin* was sinking, it was doing it very slowly. I asked if anyone had been hurt, and one man said he thought someone had been burned but he wasn't sure. (There were two fatalities.)

The seagoing tug *Chetco* finally arrived, and we backed away. We disembarked the *Etamin* men into two landing boats that came alongside and took them into the beach. By now someone on the *Etamin* had closed off watertight compartments and begun pumping out water and things were holding. It looked as though the ship would not sink and, as it turned out, it never did.

The U.S.S. *Etamin* a few days after being hit by Japanese torpedo.

For a long time after this I pondered the reactions of men in crisis situations. My first impression was that the *Etamin*'s crew had not measured up too well, because there were so many signs of panic and the scene was extremely chaotic. This initial appraisal was unfair, however. Most, if not all, of the men who scrambled in panic onto our deck were army port battalion stevedores who had been living on the *Etamin*. They had been closest to the blast. They had taken the hit and were very much in shock—which was natural—and they were scared for good reason. They knew what the *Etamin* was carrying. With all that high-octane gasoline, she was a floating bomb, apt to go off at any minute. If we had thought about that, we would have been just as frightened.

One man knew the danger, yet without hesitation came to the *Etamin*'s aid and scrambled up a rope ladder to give whatever help he could. For this act, and for his overall commendable effort in the Aitape landing, Captain John Wendell Jamison received the Legion of Merit.

Two days later the 648 escorted the *Bootes*, with the *Etamin* in tow, back to Finschhafen. At 4:45 p.m. on May 1 Captain Jamison left our ship. Before disembarking he shook hands with all three officers and commended the crew for their good performance. Jamison was a fine officer. We never knew whether he ever changed his mind about being on a "goddammed yacht" but in the two weeks aboard the 648 he made an unforgettable impression on us. In our eyes he had become our very own "General Patton."

Command

After the Aitape-Hollandia landing things again lapsed into a dreary, endless succession of convoy escorting and patrolling, still along the coast of New Guinea. In June, Spaugh wrote a letter to BuPers officially recommending me for a command. I had not requested this; in fact I tried to persuade him to wait a while longer, but by this time he was anxious to get off and get back to the States to a different type of duty. He figured as soon as the recommendation was approved he could turn command over to me—and, indeed, that's exactly what happened. On July 13, 1944, a set of orders arrived for us both, one ordering him back to SCTC for further assignment to duty and the other ordering me to take command of SC 648.

We were in Finschhafen and that night Spaugh remained on board as a passenger while we returned to Milne Bay. There, he left, without ceremony. The ship and its men became my sole responsibility as skipper. A few days prior to this Lt(jg) Woodrow W. Speier, fresh from SCTC Miami, had reported aboard to take over the duties as executive officer. Ensign Glenn F. Welsh continued in his assignment as third officer.

I had mixed feelings when Paul Spaugh left, glad to be taking over but somewhat apprehensive about certain skills that I felt were lacking in my own abilities. In the fourteen months I served under Spaugh our relationship had been quite smooth. I never experienced the feelings of animosity that had plagued Jerry because no issues of theft or missing monies arose during my tenure as executive officer. Spaugh let me conduct my duties with a minimum of interference. He, in turn, was always very decisive in ship's matters. He never gave an order that he couldn't carry out himself. He was intelligent and innovative. On more than one occasion he showed he possessed strength and courage. His biggest weakness was that of fraternizing too much with the ship's crew and occasionally, or so it seemed, playing favorites. Spaugh had no business shooting craps with the crew, but he did, and that was that. As far as I was concerned, he possessed the qualities needed to command a ship.

As for confidence in my own ability to command, I was comfortable with my relationship to the crew, and with my piloting and shiphandling skills. I was, nevertheless, somewhat uneasy with my ability in celestial navigation, primarily because I'd had so little practical experience with it. Spaugh had always done the navigating and he was good at it..

Two days after I took command we unexpectedly received orders to proceed to Cairns, Australia, for a complete overhaul. It was an overnight trip of about 250 miles across the Coral Sea—no challenge today with GPS, Loran, and other satellite-driven navigating tools-—but somewhat daunting for a new, inexperienced command with no such aids. My tools would be the sextant, a set of tables, a copy of Dutton's Navigation and some out-of-date charts. Neither Glenn Welsh nor Woody Speier were beyond classroom ability in celestial navigation so it would require my undivided attention. The crew would be testing me in other ways, also, as crews are universally apt to do.

It behooved me to plan the voyage carefully. Weather reports, such as they were, were not encouraging. Though it was fair at 2:30 p.m. when we left the anchorage at Milne Bay, by the time we reached the open sea two hours later, dark clouds were visible on the horizon. By 7:30, instead of the resplendent South Pacific sunset I had hoped for and needed in order to take sextant readings, the sky was heavy with dark, cumulus clouds and not a star in sight. The voyage would have to be made by dead reckoning. Worse, we were heading straight into a gathering sea, with salt spray and green water already coming over the bow. There was no choice but to "make a night of it" and remain with the OD in the bridge and in the chartroom. I was concerned about an atoll that lay about two-thirds of the way across and somewhat to the north of our track. It was one thing to plot a course based on speeds and compass bearings, but we would also be affected by wind and underwater currents, both unknowns.

The weather turned nasty. The southeasterly wind was gusting at 35 knots and we were heading directly into heavy seas, sending cascades of green water over the bow and scuds of spray smacking over the flying bridge. Visibility was almost zero, blacked out by low clouds and no stars.

Although everyone off watch was in his bunk, no one could sleep for the tossing and pitching. Did any of them fear whether their new skipper could get them safely to our destination? It went all night long this way, a pounding, stormy, nerve-wracking maiden voyage for a new skipper, one I've never forgotten. As I write about this today I realize my situation was tame compared with that of subchaser men who lived through the typhoons of Okinawa and elsewhere, and I look upon those sailors with genuine, open-mouthed awe.

By 5:00 a.m. things had begun lightening up. The waves had diminished some and the wind had died down a bit. There were breaks in the clouds and the sky was clearing. When I stepped outside the pilothouse I caught a glimpse of a bright star here and there. With the first faint glow of dawn I managed to get good readings on two bright stars and of all things, the moon, which was almost full. Moon sights aren't very accurate but I took one for good measure.

After working out the calculations and plotting the sextant readings I found that our fix was only two miles from our dead reckoning position! Glory be! Subchaser life wasn't so bad after all! By now a dazzling bright sun had risen and the sea was much calmer. Men stirred and came to life; Fagan recovered and made a hot breakfast for everyone. We spotted land by 11:00 a.m., and shortly after that a tanker on her way out from Cairns confirmed our position and signaled good information for traversing the Great Barrier Reef and setting a course for Cairns. By 3:00 p.m. we were nested alongside SC 699 at Smith's Landing in Cairns. Not having slept for forty-eight hours, I turned in early. I woke up in the middle of the night in a puddle, having peed in my bunk—a simple case of fatigue and the unwinding of nerves.

We were old friends with the 699, having been with her on many convoys and patrols in New Guinea. She had been inner control boat at the Biak landing in May when she got hit by a Kamikaze plane, a grueling experience. One man was killed, another missing, and eight men severely wounded. The missing man was Allen Hagmann, gunner's mate on the 648 whom we had transferred to the 699. When the plane hit he was just emerging from the engine room. His body was never found. The full story of the Kamikaze attack is told in my book "Splinter Fleet." Experts determined the 699 was salvageable and ordered her towed to Cairns for restoration and repairs. By the time we arrived she still needed another six weeks of work to restore her to fighting condition. Her skipper and exec, Hank Reentz and Phil Bash respectively, were my good friends and we managed to spend some time together.

Phil Bash

Before the war Cairns had been a sleepy coastal town, dependent primarily on sugar and fishing, but with the influx of military and naval personnel created by the fighting in New Guinea and the Solomons, Cairns began to bustle. It became a good liberty port for the crew and a nice change from New Guinea. There were movie theaters, real restaurants with pretty waitresses, and lots of fresh milk, fruits and vegetables.

One time Phil Bash and I rented some horses and spent the day ambling on dirt roads past farms, sheep ranches, fields of sugarcane and through eucalyptus groves. We saw meandering valleys between steep mountains and rode through the bushlands up onto a plateau overlooking a winding river flowing down to the sea far away. We saw lots of strange birds, including a species of crow that cawed quite differently than those in the U.S. It was a great day, a nice change from subchaser life—but oh, how stiff I was afterward!

Another day in Cairns three of us commandeered a motor launch for a cruise upriver to do some trolling. The water was as smooth as glass, winding between mountains rearing up on both sides, a picture-perfect setting that, though we netted only one king mackerel, was also a pleasant change from wartime.

We were in Cairns for three weeks, spending two days in dry dock scraping off barnacles and painting. A day of shakedown after all the repairs and another day of AA practice drills, and we were ready to return to New Guinea. We departed on August 10 with APC 15 (small coastal transport), and returned across the Coral Sea to Milne Bay under far better conditions than the voyage down. A few days later we went on to Hollandia, and for the next two and a half months we were back in the same old dreary, mind-numbing existence: Cramped, crowded, damp and as uncomfortable as ever, with endless patrol duty, or an occasional escort voyage, to Buna, Lae, or Finschhafen.

During this time we were anchored or moored almost as often as we were cruising, allowing lots of time for writing letters home, some full of blarney. I wrote one to the folks at home about life on a subchaser:

> I'm here in this hole we call the wardroom. It has the smell of sweat, after-shave lotion, and stale cigar smoke. The executive officer is in his sack opposite me studying a picture of Dorothy Woodward on the overhead and flicking his ashes into a coffee cup alongside a pair of dirty socks. Three fans are humming away rattling papers on the desk and swinging a wooden man's figure hanging from the overhead in 40° arcs. All you could wish for. We had to slip mooring alongside a nest [of ships] and anchor by ourselves, which means we won't see a movie tonight. A breeze blowing in from seaward threatens to drag anchor. It means we have to get underway and move out. Then we repeat it later, maybe twice. Right now we're by ourselves, swinging on the hook, rocking and rolling with every swell. If I want a change of atmosphere I can go up the ladder and walk about the deck dodging stanchions, stays, lanyards, cleats, hawsers, vents, hatches, goosenecks, lockers, ready boxes, guns and sailors. All this to get a breath of fresh air and take a look at hundreds of ships in this crowded harbor. I can walk up to the peak [tip of the bow], squat down and look at the anchor chain, then walk all the way aft to the fantail to check the line tied fast to our little dinghy bobbing up and down beneath me. Then I can disappear like a mole into the fetid atmosphere of the after compartment where I can duck into the galley and get a cup of java or a cold drink of

water from the scuttlebutt [water fountain]. The water tastes of chlorine and just lately diesel oil because some leaked into the water tanks recently. I can climb back up the ladder and continue forward, looking down into the engine room but refraining from going there because it's so hot and anyway I don't want to get my fingernails dirty. So I go forward into the bridge and plunk myself into the captain's chair. I light up a cigar and get engaged in conversation with the watch, keeping eyes out for the anchor dragging or fouling. I prepare the morning orders, plan the next day's work with the boatswain and think of changes in watch, quarter and station bill. I jot down some new cleaning routines and wonder who I'll get to replace the boatswain when he leaves. I check the gyro and think about our port shaft—something's wrong with both of them. I read the fuel and water report and ask gunner to give me a haircut later tonight.

It was around this time that a rare social event took place. I received an invitation from Admiral Barbey to attend a luncheon a few days hence for all Seventh Fleet Service Force ships' commanding officers. The luncheon was to be aboard his flagship, the USS *Blue Ridge*, which was anchored in Humboldt Bay, Hollandia. The invitation specified that we should wear our navy dress blues.

Well, I thought, this is a pleasant surprise—lunch with the admiral, eh? Better get out my navy blues, shirt, and tie and shine up my shoes and look proper. This was easier said than done, however, for when I unzipped my blue uniform from the duffle bag it was badly wrinkled and spotted here and there with a grayish mold. Beck helped me clean it up with a lot of brushing and I hung it out in the sun for a day so it didn't look too bad. We didn't have any starch but at least my shirt was clean

The day came and a launch from the *Blue Ridge* went around Humboldt harbor collecting the skippers from each ship. Ours must have been the only subchaser in port that day because no one I knew was at the luncheon. There must have been seventy-five officers altogether, most of them lieutenant commanders or above. The luncheon was held in the *Blue Ridge's* wardroom, which was laid out like a fancy dining salon for the occasion. Admiral Barbey stood at the doorway with three or four staff officers and they greeted each of us with a handshake. I felt conspicuously outranked but it didn't matter.

Trays with goblets of wine were offered and we stood around in small groups sipping and introducing ourselves. The tables were set up family style, draped with white linen set neatly with silver flatware and cloth napkins arranged fanlike at each place. Stewards and mess attendants in starched white jackets stood by. I couldn't help thinking what a stark contrast this was to the eating arrangements on my little subchaser.

Once seated, I found myself between a navy tanker captain on my right and a commander of an AKA transport on my left. The latter had an old buddy seated next to him and the two of them talked and swapped stories during the entire luncheon. The captain of the tanker on my right was a cold type who, after learning I commanded a subchaser, virtually ignored me and conversed most of the time with the guest on his right.

As the luncheon progressed I heard someone say the word "subchaser." An officer down the table on the opposite side was telling his table companion about a subchaser he had recently been aboard as a passenger. He was saying things like "You wouldn't believe it ... crowded ... unbelievable ... smelly ... cramped . . cockroaches ... don't know how they stand it." He was describing what could have been my ship! As I listened I thought, well, at least subchasers are interesting enough to talk about. I almost felt smug. I knew more than he did about subchasers; and even if they were the lowliest of low in the navy's pecking order, I had the finest subchaser in the whole damn navy. At that moment I felt nothing but pride in my ship and my men.

Halfway through the luncheon a black mess attendant (in those days, the vast majority of black people didn't serve in the navy in any other capacity than stewards and mess boys) leaned over between my chair and the captain's chair on my right to retrieve a water pitcher. In doing this he apparently brushed the captain's shoulder.

The captain exploded. "Damn you!" he said angrily, glaring up at the mess attendant. "Don't you ever do that again!" With his napkin he wiped his shoulder in angry jabs where the mess attendant had touched him. Talking stopped, people stared. Shaken, the beleaguered, perspiring attendant retreated.

The captain turned back to his plate. "Damn niggers have no place in the navy," he grumbled aloud to no one in particular. I had never witnessed such arrogance, hatred, and insensitivity. It shocked and angered me. I should have challenged him, or at least removed myself from the table. Shamefully, I said and did nothing—like everyone else who heard the outburst.

The admiral's luncheon, though well intentioned, made a lasting impression on me, but for all the wrong reasons. The old cliché "loneliness of command" was quite real that day aboard the Blue Ridge.

I wish I had known Admiral Dan Barbey personally. His book "MacArthur's Amphibious Navy" describes in great detail the Seventh Amphibious Force landing operations that we were in, and it's obvious he was a very human, regular guy, a quality I had not perceived among many men in the higher echelons. On our subchasers we knew nothing about where we were going or what to expect at the time. Sixty years later it's nice to be able to catch up and put things in perspective. Of course I could have done this long before, but that's what resulted from putting the navy behind me. Writing this book has forced me to do some research to find out where I was going and why.

For instance, in "MacArthur's Amphibious Navy" the admiral explains why, after securing Hollandia, we didn't go directly to the Philippines. Hollandia had become an immense staging area, ideal for launching an assault, or so it would appear. Instead, we made additional landings at smaller islands like Biak, Wakde, Moratai, and Saidor. Every major commander in the Southwest Pacific had moved his headquarters to Hollandia. Good roads, wooden barracks, and Quonset huts blossomed overnight. Tent cities dotted the landscape and the harbor filled with hundreds of ships. Why couldn't we have bypassed those other islands? From Barbey we learn that soil conditions in Hollandia made it incapable of holding up under heavy bomber operations. There was an urgent need to find a site that could support land-based planes of all types. The closest American bomber base was more than 400 miles to the rear and we had to get closer. With the smaller islands finally secured, General MacArthur's dream of returning to the Philippines came to fruition. End of history lesson.

Leyte

On October 20, 1944, the greatest invading force ever assembled in the Pacific was launched against Leyte. The battle took seven weeks of almost continuous fighting on land, on sea, and in the air. Historian Samuel Eliot Morison describes it as "the greatest naval battle of all time."

On the 648 the voyage to Leyte began on November 7 when we departed from Hollandia in company with DE 635 (USS *England*), OTC, and SCs 637, 698, 731, 745, 749, 734, and 748. Our job was to escort a slow-moving convoy of Army FS boats with tows, joined later by three tugs with tows. "Slow-moving" meant speeds ranging from three to six knots; therefore, the trip from Hollandia took almost two weeks, twice as long as normal. Two times during the voyage we had to take on fuel, water, and provisions from an Army tanker.

Anyone who has tethered hoses to a giant ship for purposes of taking on fuel while both vessels are underway knows how ticklish this can be, especially if the weather acts up or the water is rough. We had some nervous moments during these fuelings, but fortunately there were no mishaps. Twelve days after leaving Hollandia we moored alongside SC 745 in San Pedro Bay, Leyte. By this time the big naval battles around Leyte had been fought and won. For Japan, the battles of Surigao Strait, Samar, and Cape Engano, involving dozens of carriers, cruisers, and other large warships—critical turning points in the Pacific war—were crushing defeats.

These U.S. victories followed the initial assault on Leyte and gave us complete control of air and sea power. Nevertheless, the enemy, though badly depleted, continued to harass shipping in and around Leyte Gulf, mostly with high-altitude bombing raids. Day and night during our month at Leyte we were under a Red Alert or at General Quarters. Red Alerts were radioed warnings to be prepared for an air attack. The warnings were issued when bogies [enemy aircraft] were spotted on someone's radar screen, although we generally didn't come to battle stations unless word spread that an attack was imminent. The attacks came mostly at night. Lacking radar on the 648, we'd man our stations and wait until we heard a broadcast to secure, or, as happened frequently, shooting started. It took only one ship to commence firing before the entire armada followed, in a deafening, never-to-be-forgotten display of fireworks. Tracers [fifth shell in every round] crisscrossed the sky in an overwhelming wall of firepower. You'd know a plane got hit when you saw a bright puff of smoke or fire. Searchlight beams would train on it and all ships would commence firing. At eight or ten thousand feet up, the stricken plane would seem to fall very slowly, all the while under heavy, concentrated fire. Sometimes when it was happening you'd think about the men killed or dying in that plane. Enemies, true, but with families or sweethearts waiting at home for their safe return. Fortunately, there wasn't time to dwell obsessively on such matters. The ships were often too slow to cease firing. By the time the plane hit the water, the tracers were horizontal and the ships were shooting at each other. When this happened we'd hear frantic messages on the radio: "CRAW-

FISH from HAYSTACK (each ship had a code name), you're shooting through my rigging" or "Cease firing, man wounded." Fortunately, it never happened to us, although a spent shell once fell on our ship.

There were daytime raids, too, which had their own element of excitement, even humor. Shortly after we arrived in Leyte, gunner Green acquired a monkey from one of the many outrigger canoes trading for cigarettes. The monkey, a rhesus, was the size of a skunk, a typical "organ grinder" type monkey who won the hearts of the crew and quickly adapted to shipboard life. Green named her Josephine in honor of an aunt and we called her "Josie."

One morning Jap Zeros came in and everyone took stations at general quarters. As skipper, my station was on the flying bridge. We had them in our sights as they came over our bow, from port to starboard, 1,500 feet high. We opened fire with several other ships, our 40 mm gun pom-pomming and the 20 mm guns tat-tatting in fine fettle, making lots of noise. In the middle of this I felt something sharp on the back of my bare leg. It was Josie, terrified, hanging on so hard I couldn't shake her off. Only when the shooting stopped did she relax her grip and when she did my leg felt warm and wet all over. In her panic she had peed on my leg. We didn't get any planes that time but I got kidded quite a bit.

Josie, ship's pet, keeps a sharp lookout on the bow

At Leyte, as everywhere else, subchasers often tied together in nests, utilizing one vessel's anchor for as many as four or five, since mooring was easier than anchoring. One morning a Red Alert sounded, calling everyone to general quarters. We were in a nest with the 738 moored to our starboard side. Her gun crew was on station, her cannon trained with its muzzle directly over the heads of our 40 mm gun crew. In the Pacific most subchasers by now had converted to a 40 mm forward gun because the 3-inch 50 cannon was suitable only for shooting at a surface craft. It was too slow and unwieldy for fighting aircraft and was very noisy when it went off. The 738 was still awaiting conversion.

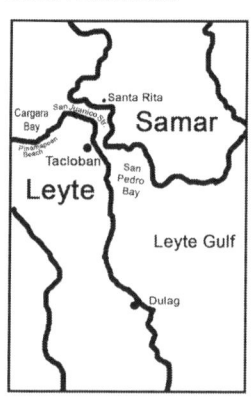

Both subchasers had their battle stations manned and ready for Jap planes if they came. We waited several minutes with no sightings until I was beginning to think it was another false alarm, when suddenly, BANG! The 738's cannon let go. Her pointer had accidentally tripped either the foot control or the electric control. The concussion knocked our gun crew off their seats and stations and sent them sprawling on the deck. Fortunately, there was only one injury, a ruptured eardrum in one of our gunners, Gale Cox. Lots of feelings were ruffled and a few curses directed at the 738. As for the Red Alert? No planes showed up that time.

One day we were on our way out of San Pedro Bay for a day of patrolling when we spotted a subchaser 2,000 yards ahead looking dead in the water. She was down by the stern, her fantail flush with the water. As we drew closer I recognized her as the SC 744. Her skipper, Don Stroetzel, was a good friend, one of the officers with whom I had played poker the night before.

Main Street Tacloban, Leyte, November 1944

When we got near, Don and three of his crew were on the flying bridge. The 744 had been struck earlier that day by a Jap Kamikaze plane while escorting a tug with barge in tow on their way to the western side of Leyte. The dead and wounded and most of the crew had been removed and they were waiting for a tug on the way to tow them back to Tacloban. When I asked whether he needed anything, he said the 749 had come by and given them food and an extra billy pump. Wishing him well, we continued on our way. (The story of the attack is told in Chapter 18 of "Splinter Fleet".)

SC 744 shortly after being struck by a Japanese Kamikaze plane November 27, 1944 in Leyte Gulf. Picture taken by someone on the navy tug TP 114. Courtesy of Al Angelini, PhM1C, a survivor of the attack. Al is still living in California.

I've mentioned more than once that subchasers were as low as you could get in the navy's pecking order but to someone on an LCT, life on a subchaser was like being in the lap of luxury. Ungainly, uncomfortable, and hard to maneuver, the LCTs and the other smaller landing craft were little more than power-driven barges, yet the flat-bottomed "scows" and their men were in the lion's jaw of most landing operations. They fought bad weather, heavy surf, and enemy fire, but delivered the goods with little thanks.

On one occasion we escorted four LCTs through the San Juanico Straits, a narrow waterway separating the northeast end of Leyte from the southwest corner of Samar, the adjoining island. Our job was to guide them through the straits, across Cargara Bay to a point at Pinamapoan where they could beach and unload tanks for supporting the troops fighting inland. As the only escort, we were like a mother duck leading four ugly ducklings. Traversing the straits should have been an afternoon "cruisin' down the river" if it weren't for the threat of sniper fire. Dense foliage on both sides provided perfect cover for snipers, so we wore battle helmets, carried sidearms, and stayed alert. At several points we passed crude wooden docks behind which were huts with supposedly friendly people, but we could never be sure.

Tracer fire lights up the sky as ships fire their AA guns on enemy night raiders. This photo was taken at Okinawa but the same scene was enacted nightly at Leyte. National Archives (127GR Box 15)

After passing through the straits we headed for a point across the bay at Pinamapoan beach, keeping a sharp eye on our little brood of LCTs. They had a tendency to stray from formation. One was having engine trouble, making it necessary to slow to 5 knots. The weather was wet and humid with low clouds hanging over. Halfway across the bay we ran into a rain squall that reduced visibility to 50 feet. I slowed, signaling the LCT immediately astern of us to close and to tell the others to do the same. They floundered about, going in four different directions. It took an hour of circling around and hollering through a megaphone before we were able to corral them together again. The squall ended as abruptly as it began and soon we were at the beach. The LCTs unloaded, and two hours later we were on our way back through the San Juanico Straits.

Having left Tacloban with orders to depart as quickly as possible, we had no time to top off our fresh water supply. I decided to stop at Santa Rita, a village halfway through the straits on the Samar side, to replenish our fresh water tanks. Signalling the LCTs to heave to and wait, we tied up  at a small dock at Santa Rita. A crowd of native Filipinos gathered at the dock with poultry, eggs, bananas, and other foods for sale or trade. A man introduced himself to me and said he was the mayor. In broken English he spoke about the mistreatment they had received from the Japs and how glad they were that the Americans were back in the Phillipines. He introduced a couple of teenaged boys he said were his nephews. The boys seemed quite interested in the ship. They whispered something to their uncle and he relayed to me that they were asking if they could come aboard. They wanted to be able to tell their friends they had been on a real U.S. navy warship. Glenn Welsh took them in tow and showed them around. One of the LCTs moored at the dock and the others dropped anchors and waited. Half a dozen more Filipinos came aboard, engaging the crew in conversation and light trading.

Glenn Welsh came back from the "tour" with the two boys, who began talking earnestly with their uncle, the mayor. He told me they wanted to stay aboard as part of the crew. The idea was unthinkable for obvious reasons. But Glenn and Woodie and a couple of crew members picked up on the idea, commenting on how we could use some additional help in the galley. The mayor sent for the boys' father, who, after being summoned to the dock, vouchsafed his consent. To this day it's hard for me to believe I allowed it—or to admit I allowed it—but that's probably why I ended up serving in the "Donald Duck Navy." We made our own rules as we went along. I figured it would be easy enough to return the boys if they didn't work out. With many expressions of goodwill, farewell hugs, and hand waving, we shoved off from the dock at Santa Rita with Jack and Joe newly added to our ship's company.

Jack and Joe

One week after that we received orders to return to Hollandia. There was no time to return Jack and Joe to Santa Rita. I had to settle for taking them along, figuring we could return them later, assuming that our return to Leyte was inevitable, which it wasn't.

Waifs of war, Tacloban P.I.

Store front, Tacloban P.I

Our 40mm gun crew

The Lifeboat

We were in Leyte for a month. Everyone was ready for a change. Morale was poor, nerves were frayed, the mail was always slow. There'd been no R & R, no liberties. Several men were expecting orders for transfer back to the States. I'd been out there almost two years. Twenty-one months of that time had been on the 648. I'd had enough sea duty for a while. Most SC officers served twelve to eighteen months and then returned to the States. They'd have thirty days of leave, then go back to SCTC to be instructors, or take command of a larger ship such as a PC (173-foot steel-hulled patrol craft) or a DE (289-foot steel-hulled "small destroyer"). Many of these ultimately returned to the Pacific. I wondered why I hadn't been called back to stateside. Why had I heard nothing from BuPers about a relief on the way?

It was time for me to have a change of duty. The green ensign, the ignoramus, the starry-eyed dreamer who pictured himself "on the high seas shooting at the enemy in glorious combat" had matured. Thanks to the navy I was much more sensible and realistic—but not infallible.

To return to Hollandia was nothing to celebrate but at least it would be a change of scenery; there would be less pressure and fewer threats of Kamikazes, and our mail situation would improve. On December 15, 1944 we left Leyte in a convoy of twenty-six ships escorted by three destroyers, two frigates, one DE, and the 648. One of the destroyers was the USS *Lamson* (DD 367), which had taken a direct hit from a Kamikaze at Ormoc Bay ten days before. Twenty-one of her men had been killed and her ensign flew at half mast. We were the only subchaser, the smallest ship in the convoy.

The voyage back was without incident other than with Jack and Joe, the Filipino boys, who got so seasick they lay in their bunks the entire trip and proved worthless. It turned out they were of no help whether at sea or in port.

The day before we were to make landfall at Hollandia one of the lead destroyers flashed us with her signal lamp. After we acknowledged, she sent the following message:

> Little fellow please retrieve small boat adrift three thousand yards ahead of you and take in tow.

Through our binoculars we saw a grey speck bobbing on the surface. Drawing closer, we could see that it was an empty 21-foot double-ended motor lifeboat in fine condition. Its boathook and oars were neatly lashed down and miscellaneous tools, water, and provisions were stored in lockers under the seats. There were numbers painted on its stern and it appeared to be the type of lifeboat carried by Liberty ships. (Liberty ships were 10,000-ton cargo ships built assembly-line style from prefabricated sections. More than 2,700 Liberty ships were built during the war.) We took the lifeboat in tow as ordered and I told Beebe to signal the destroyer to let them know we had it.

Everyone admired the boat as she rode high in our wake. Someone said, "Boy, we could sure use a boat." Several months earlier we had lost our little wherry in a storm and we missed it badly. A boat was indispensable when we were at anchor, our only means for getting around the harbor and into the beach for mail, food, and supplies. Without a boat we had to beg rides no matter how small or routine, making it inconvenient, time-wasting, and demeaning.

I stood on the flying bridge looking at it. How great it would be for the 648 to have a boat like that! Beebe received another message from the destroyer:

Because we saw the boat first we claim salvage rights.

Salvage rights? The message tweaked something in my memory. Hadn't I heard once that when you find something on the high seas you have a legal right to ownership—something called salvage rights? The destroyer skipper was kidding, so I sent him a reply:

Sorry, but finders keepers.

Van Kirk and Beebe began pressing. "Cap'n," Van Kirk said, "We need that boat more than that Liberty ship does. They probably got seven more like it. Anyway, they must be pretty stupid to lose a boat. They don't deserve it."

"Yeah, Cap'n," chimed in Beebe, "Think of all those times we've needed a boat. All the other SCs have boats. Why can't we?"

Other crewmen clustered around talking about it.

"It's time we had a boat, Cap'n," said George Green. "Hell, if you keep it I'll be your personal coxswain."

"No, I want that job," said Gale Cox.

"Yeah, you've got the name for it," someone added.

"No kiddin', Cap'n, you should keep that boat."

"We really need it, Cap'n."

They were all talking at once.

"Pipe down," I said. "Wait a minute. If we keep that boat someone's bound to show up and claim it."

"So what? We found it on the open sea. How can they claim it? Too bad if they lost their boat. Anyone who loses a boat doesn't deserve it in the first place. We recovered it. It would have been lost if we hadn't picked it up."

I was thinking we could get more done and save lots of time with a boat. With no hassle, either. Morale was low. Leyte hadn't been easy. The men were getting into needless arguments. Two years out there may have matured me but I was still impetuous.

"All right, we'll try keeping it and see what happens," I said, knowing there could be some trouble over it but if someone from the Liberty ship showed up it would be easy enough to give it back. There'd be nothing lost and a lot to gain because we really needed a boat, we'd get good use out of it, and it would be a great boost for morale.

When we arrived in Hollandia on December 21 I had the men stow all the boat's gear in the lazarette except for items necessary to operate it. I told them not to paint over anything or try to disguise the boat, for I didn't want to be accused of concealment if or when someone came to claim it. The boat's very first errand was to pick up the long-awaited mail. When Green returned with five sacks of new mail the morale problem was solved, at least for the time being. We had our mail and we had us a boat!

We used it for all kinds of errands. Some of the other subchasers were without boats and we helped them with their errands. The boat became the pride and joy of Green, Cox, and Keltner, who kept it in top-notch condition. How had we ever gotten along without it? Supplies, food, engine parts, stores, ammunition—these things were easy now. The boat was in constant use. The men took turns operating it and they were good at it. The only problem was that the boat was too big to haul aboard in case we were ordered to sea for escort or patrol duty. Since we were in port for an overhaul this seemed unlikely for a while, however.

Christmas in Hollandia in 1944 was not much different from any other day except for the nice turkey dinner. We had all the fixings, thanks to Pete Malloy, a Harvard classmate, who was supply officer on our tender, USS *Fulton*. Fagan was long gone by now, and two successive ship's cooks hadn't worked out, so it was up to Glenn McFall, a young seaman, who was filling in until a new ship's cook caught up with us. He did a very creditable job.

On the day after Christmas we received orders to proceed to Manus Island in the Admiralties for our overhaul—an unexpected turn of events, for we had believed we would be in Hollandia undergoing overhaul for quite some time. Hollandia, it seems, was backed up with too many vessels requiring repairs. Facilities at Manus were available to take the overflow. We faced the problem of either leaving our lifeboat in Hollandia or towing it to Manus. Luckily, the orders were for us to steam alone, independently, so I decided we could tow it over to Manus.

On December 28 we arrived at Manus without incident, the lifeboat still a part of our ship's gear. Again we settled into the routine of being moored or anchored, but now we had the boat and it got plenty of use.

A week or so after arriving in Manus I left the ship one morning to attend to some business ashore. When I returned at noon, three men were standing on the 648's quarterdeck. They had been waiting for me. One of them, short and thin, wore a merchant marine officer's cap. He accosted me.

"Are you the captain of this ship?"

"Yes sir," I replied, knowing full well who he was.

"Well, I'm the master of the SS *Thomas P. Leathers* and you have a boat back there that belongs to us."

"Oh?" I said, "We do have a boat back there but it's our boat."

His face reddened. "That's our boat. It's off our ship. It got loose in a storm. It's our boat and I can prove it."

"I'm sorry," I said, "it's our boat. What makes you think you have a right to it?"

His face darkened. "You've got some nerve saying that's your boat. I can prove it's my boat. I've got papers to prove it."

I knew I was wrong but I wasn't going to let my men see me give it up without a fight.

"Look," I said, "I don't care what you've got. It's our boat. If you think that's your boat you're going to have to do more than just tell me it's yours. That boat belongs to us until someone proves otherwise."

He was furious.

"I'll sure as hell show you whose boat that is. I'll be back and you can be goddam sure of that!" Turning, he stalked off the ship with the two other men, muttering obscenities.

Woody and Glenn and some of the men gathered around.

"Doesn't look too good, does it?" said Woody.

"Oh, he's just blowing smoke," I said. "We may lose it but we'll stick it out a while longer"

The devil-may-care attitude was something new in my persona. The long months of island hopping, patrols, red alerts, Kamikazes, and sheer weariness were getting to me. Apparently, using today's terminology, I was burned out. I didn't give a damn about some things. We needed that boat and we'd gotten things done with it. You had to fight for things there. This little man from the merchant marine wasn't going to push me around and that was that.

Next morning I was in the wardroom writing a letter when someone called down from above: "Captain, you've got company up here!"

The three men from the Liberty ship were standing on the quarterdeck. With them was a big sailor in neat whites with a Shore Patrol band on his arm and a billy club on his belt. He saluted me and said, "Sir, these men are claiming that boat back there belongs to them, that it cast loose from their ship."

"Maybe so," I replied, "But we found and recovered that boat in open waters. It was abandoned and adrift. As far as we know it belongs to no one other than who found it. We have salvage rights to that boat."

The merchant mariner was livid. He held up a sheaf of papers. "I can prove it's our boat. I have the papers. I can show you the numbers. They'll match up."

The SP said, "Sir, I have to go back and check the numbers with him."

I said, "Sure, go ahead. Take your time."

They went back to the boat and when they returned the SP asked to speak to me alone.

"Sir," he said, "I checked their numbers and they match the numbers on the boat. There's no doubt the boat is off their ship and you're going to have to turn it over to them. I know where you're coming from, sir, but I have to tell you that if you don't let them have it I'll have to take you over to the port director where you can tell your side of the story. But I can tell you the port director won't let you get away with it and you'll end up having to return the boat anyway and it might stir up some shit and you could have a real problem. It would be better all around if you'd just turn the boat over to them and let it go, and that would be the end of it."

Naturally, he was right and I had to back off. No sense in being too devil-may-care.

"OK, sailor, you make sense, they can have it."

I had my men take the gear they had stored in the lazarette and put it back in the boat. I watched as the three men climbed into the boat making ready to get underway. The merchant captain was going through everything, looking for missing items. He was seething.

"There's stuff missing," he said.

"Take it easy," I said. "Be thankful you're getting it back. We're giving you everything we found."

They shoved off. The captain stood in the boat still furious. Moving out, he shouted some obscenities aimed at me, concluding with "You haven't heard the end of this!"

Burnout

My staleness, burnout, or whatever it could be, was exacerbated with a yearning to see Zan Ward in Toledo. Her letters, which I eagerly awaited and read many times over, were an escape from the reality of our life on the dirty, wet, cramped little subchaser. They reminded me of all the good things back home and the way life could and should be, once we got this frigging war behind us. I began thinking of her in a more romantic way, not just as a pen pal. Our letters had been getting more personal of late. When one of her letters closed with "Love" instead of the usual "Best regards," I made certain my reply closed with "Love" also. Not long after this I somewhat audaciously began a letter with the salutation "Dearest Zan" instead of "Dear Zan" and then worried through three weeks for her reply. When it finally came and I read "Dearest Ted," I felt as though she had kissed me. I began to fantasize about her. I wrote a letter that closed with "Lots of love" instead of the single word "Love." She responded with "Lots of love" also. That hurdle overcome, I tried "Love and Kisses." Evidently this was too fast, because her reply remained as before, "Lots of love." That's the way she was. She kept the relationship sensible and honest, the way it had to be.

Almost five years had gone by since I had last seen her, but I had always remembered the soft glow in her eyes when she brought me sandwiches while I was painting her father's cottage. Even then I had thought she'd make a good wife for someone someday. Now, with each letter from her, I found myself wanting to see her more than ever. I was impatient for my relief to arrive and told the yeoman to keep his eyes open for a letter from BuPers saying he was on his way. I began dreaming of the day when I would actually once more be in the United States. The first thing I would do would be to phone my parents in New Jersey. Then I would phone Zan for an invitation to stop there on the way east. I wasn't exactly sure what I had in mind except I had to do it.

We were still undergoing overhaul and in some ways it was worse than being at sea. We were getting tired of always having to forage for things and there was little to do for R & R. The men played softball with other subchasers at a makeshift playing field, and once in a while we'd get out the gloves and do a little sparring. Card games, reading, writing letters, or sacking out were the only other activities. One day a U.S.O. group came through and put on a show on land with John Wayne and some Hollywood starlets. Another time I sat near the stage that had been set up on the deck of an aircraft carrier. An officer I didn't know was sitting on my right. I was smoking a cigar. A puff of wind blew a big ash from the cigar all over the officer, startling him. I apologized and helped brush off the ashes and he was good about it. A few minutes later the announcer introduced Lanny Ross to the crowd and this officer stood up and went to the microphone and began singing. Lanny Ross was a well-known, popular tenor of the times. I don't recall any other famous stage or screen personalities while we were out there.

The protracted period of inactivity led to boredom and malaise. The men needed things to keep busy, things to keep their minds off their homesickness. I decided the ship could use some sprucing up. The forward crew's compartment was especially dirty and grungy and it smelled bad. I ordered Green to get a couple of his deck hands and give it a thorough cleaning and painting. What followed is best told in a letter sent to me fifty years later from his brother, gunner Jay Green:

George wasn't easy ... you wanted to clean and paint up the ship. It was looking pretty sloppy. You told Green to have the forward crew's quarters painted. Green asked "Any particular color?" You answered, "The bulkheads should be white, the foot lockers and upright lockers can be any color you like" Of course that gave George an opening for some of his creative genius. So George told each of us to paint white on the bulkheads around our individual bunks. Then he said we were going to have the most outstanding forward compartment in the U.S.Navy. He said he had found some stripping paint in the paint locker and he didn't know what it was ever used for. So we'd use it here on the foot lockers and upright lockers. The only thing he suggested was that we each use a different color. He figured you had given him a leeway when you said "Paint them any colors you want".

When the job was finished the footlockers were painted every color of the rainbow. Then, on the door of the head, which was up forward, he painted a gamecock—a beautiful job. George was quite an artist. And under the gamecock's rear end he put a pile of brown mess. After all the painting was finished he asked you to come down and inspect it. I'm sure you remember. You came down, looked around, didn't say anything about the footlockers, but when George showed you the door of the head with the gamecock painted on it you looked at it for a minute, then you said, "Green, the chicken can stay, but the shit's got to go." Everyone in there that day was completely fooled. We thought you would blow your stack. Did you know we had a lot of people from the other ships come over just to see that colorful compartment?

George Green was a good man and a hard worker. He and Jay were two of our best men, although quite different in makeup and personality. George had a great sense of Yankee humor but at times was argumentative and contrary. Jay was always even-tempered. They were both loyal and competent and I had a high regard for each of them. George Green outdid himself with that painting job. Everything looked spanking new and bright. The bright colors, bizarre and un-navy to the core, made the compartment look like a children's classroom—or maybe a Salvador Dali exhibit room. When I got topside I couldn't help laughing. The objectionable part was painted over and the chicken remained—at least for the remainder of my time on the ship. Some skippers would probably have had Green up for a captain's mast for insubordination.

Impatient to get off the ship and back to the States, on January 1, 1945, I wrote a Speedletter to the Chief of Naval Operations:

> REQUEST THIRTY DAY LEAVE IN U.S. AND ASSIGNMENT NEW CONSTRUCTION OR DIFFERENT TYPE DUTY. HAVE COMPLETED TWENTY TWO MONTHS OVERSEAS DUTY. TWENTY MONTHS ABOARD THIS VESSEL. SIX MONTHS AS COMMANDING OFFICER. PHYSICALLY AND MENTALLY FATIGUED. PRESENT EXECUTIVE OFFICER WELL QUALIFIED FOR COMMAND. ENSIGN REQUIRED FOR RELIEF. APPLICATION MILITARY GOVERNMENT SCHOOL FORWARDED 7 AUGUST 1944. NO REPLY YET.

The reference to Military Government School refers to a request I had made in July in response to a directive inviting reserve officers to consider a career in the navy, with postwar assignments to a foreign country. The higher-ups realized that victory over the Axis and Japan would require considerable adjustment for the defeated countries and for a while I actually considered making a career with the navy for this purpose. I was only a year below the minimum age requirement and it was near the cutoff date for applications and was subsequently turned down.

Finally, on January 17th came the message from BuPers in typical navy style:

LT THEODORE TREADWELL JR DVG USNR 134093 X DISPATCH ORDERS 151556 NOV REPEATED FOR COMPLIANCE X RELDET [Relative to detachment] BY LT JG JOHN WILLIAM STORRS JR DVG USNR DUTY CO X PROCEED PORT US THENCE PROREP [Proceed and report] NAVTRACEN [Naval Training Center] MIAMI FLA TEMDUINS [Temporary duty under instruction] FURASPERS [Further assignment Personnel] X DELREP [Delay reporting] ONE MONTH

Two weeks later, on February 2nd to be exact, Lt(jg) John W. Storrs arrived to relieve me of command. Storrs, fresh from SCTC Miami, was almost as excited to be taking over as I was to be relieved.

Whenever a ship's command changes there are inspections, lots of authorizations, and papers to sign. To his credit, Storrs did a thorough job, taking the better part of the day asking questions and making a thorough inspection of the entire ship. In the forward compartment, freshly painted in George Green's myriad colors, Storrs looked around while I waited for a reaction, but there was none. All he said was, "Hmmm, interesting."

Later that day, Storrs and I sat down in the wardroom. He said, "Captain, everything looks pretty good, but there's a problem."

"A problem? What's that?"

"Those two Filipino kids. Captain, in all honesty I simply can't take over the ship with those two aboard. I cannot risk that responsibility."

I tried to make light of it. "Oh, they're no problem. You'll be going back to Leyte soon enough. It'll be easy enough, and you can let them go when you get up there."

"I can't do it, Captain. I can't take any chances. They don't belong on the ship and I simply cannot take over with them aboard. I'm not signing anything as long as they're on board."

He was right and I knew it.

"Well, OK, I'll just have to find someone to take them," I said. "There won't be any problem. You'll be back first thing tomorrow?" He was billeted at the BOQ in Manus.

"Oh, sure, I'll be back first thing in the morning." We shook hands and he left.

I was confident that I could find somebody to take Jack and Joe back to Leyte, but after asking several skippers and getting refused, I began to worry. Most of them had good reasons for not taking them, mainly because they didn't know where they would be sent next. They might never return to Leyte, for all they knew. I finally asked Bob MacLean, skipper of SC 734, a man I had never known very well, if he'd be willing. Without hesitating he said, "Sure, no problem." Whew! He took the two boys early the next morning and I was able to satisfy Storrs. The act of compliance (compassion?) made Bob MacLean "my kind of guy." I never saw him again, but wherever he is I owe him one.

On February 3rd John Storrs officially relieved me of my first and only command. There were no special ceremonies, no formalities, no dramatics. I packed my belongings, said goodbye to several individual members of the crew, and departed, leaving a little bit of myself on that unkempt little warthog of a subchaser. You can't live aboard a ship for twenty-three months without developing a strange, inexplicable affection for her. She had taken me safely through all kinds of water, all kinds of weather, and all kinds of situations bad and good alike. She was a stout ship, a seagoing ship, a tough little warrior. I didn't feel like this as much then as I do today for I was too excited at the thought of finally returning home.

Home

I returned to the States as a passenger on SS *Wideawake*, a Liberty ship. The voyage took twenty-two days and was memorable for good food and poker games with a group of fighter pilots on their way home. They kept talking about the ship being so slow. All of us were in a state of exhilaration. The battle of Iwo Jima was in full swing.

On February 26 the *Wideawake* moored alongside a dock at Terminal Island, Longbeach, California. Walking down the gangway I could hardly believe I was once again stepping on U.S. soil, and it felt exhilarating. On the *Wideawake* I had gotten friendly with a fellow passenger, a grizzled career-navy warrant officer whose real name I can't remember but for this story I'll call him Ziggy. He accompanied me down the gangway and we arranged to find a hotel and share a room for overnight, after which we'd go our separate ways. I can't remember the name of the hotel, but as soon as we got in the room I wasted no time calling my parents and Zan and my brother, Dave, who by now lived in Richland, Washington. I arranged to visit Dave before flying east.

Ziggy and I took hot showers and got dressed in our navy blues, Ziggy's with many service stripes and ribbons with stars adorning his chest. We then found a nice-looking restaurant, knowing exactly what we wanted. The waiter seated us and we ordered whiskies and water. We looked over the menu but couldn't find beef or steak dishes listed. We called the waiter over and told him we wanted to order a couple of T-bone steaks smothered in onions.

The waiter said, "I'm sorry, but we have no steaks."

"No steaks, how come?"

"Gentlemen, there's a war going on. I'm sorry, but no one has steak any more.

Ziggy said, "What's your name, waiter?"

"Roland, sir."

"Roland, you look like a nice guy, but listen up for a moment. The two of us have just come from the worst fighting in the whole damn Pacific. This gentleman," nodding to me, "had his ship sunk under him in the Battle of Leyte. He personally saved seven crew members who would have died were it not for him. I know, because I was one of them. And I'll tell you something more. He's been recommended for the Congressional Medal of Honor, the highest honor anyone can get. We just got back this afternoon. I promised this gentleman—this war hero—that as soon as we landed I would take him to the first nice restaurant I could find and treat him to the best T-bone steak dinner he ever had. Think about it. Roland, you wouldn't want to make a liar out of me, would you?"

Roland looked flustered.

"If you would please, sir, excuse me, I'll speak to the manager." He left the table.

It was hard to keep a straight face. "What the hell did you say that for?" I hissed. "You crazy?"

The waiter returned with the manager, a neatly dressed individual.

"Gentlemen," he said, "So you've just returned from the Pacific, eh, and you want steaks? We used to serve the finest steak dishes in the area but we can't get beef anymore. I'm sorry, but we haven't served steaks here for over a year."

Ziggy looked at him in disbelief.

"You mean to say you have no beef in your locker? Did Roland here tell you about this man sitting across from me? About how he saved my life from a sinking ship and how he's being awarded the Congressional Medal of

Honor? And how I promised him I'd buy him the finest T-bone steak as soon as we got back? Which was the very least I could do under the circumstances, don't you think?"

The manager studied us for a good fifteen seconds, then, "Gentlemen, where there's a will there's a way." He whispered something in Roland's ear, then said, "Gentlemen, we'll take care of it. Just tell Roland here how you want your steaks."

They were delicious.

After we had finished, and savoring another drink, we looked at each other. Ziggy read my mind. He said, "Let's have another." He called for the waiter.

Roland blinked, but took the order and returned to the kitchen.

We had another drink while waiting.

The second T-bones came and we ate them just as greedily as the first, but we'd slowed down a bit. When I finally got up from the table I realized all was not well. I headed straight for the men's room and threw up both steaks and most of the liquor. Ziggy did likewise. Gluttony had its reward, and that was ours.

The next day I flew to Seattle to visit Dave and his family. It had been a long time since I had seen him and this was a good opportunity to catch up with family matters. From Seattle I took a bus to Pasco, where Dave picked me up for the drive to Richland. He greeted me warmly, looking about the same as always.

As we rode along he seemed preoccupied so I tried to make conversation.

"I know you're still working for DuPont, but what are you doing out here? Probably making something for the war effort, no doubt?"

He merely nodded.

I said, "Well, what are you making?"

He said, "Listen. I don't want you asking me a lot of questions. I get up very early in the morning and leave the house at quarter to six. I drive fifty miles to where I work. I don't get home until seven p.m. or later, and that's all. As to what I do and what DuPont or anyone else is doing, it's nobody's business—and that includes you. I will not talk about it and neither will you, OK?" He was dead serious.

"Well, certainly, of course," I murmured. Big brother always had the last say and that was the end of that.

I spent two days and nights catching up and getting acquainted with my little niece Martha and nephews David II and Anthony. They lived in a huge development of prefabricated houses, a community of more than 30,000 people that had mushroomed almost overnight in the windswept desert area of eastern Washington. All the husbands worked on a top-secret project somewhere 50 miles away while the wives socialized and raised their young families. Something big was taking place but I was not privy to it. I stayed in Richland about three days. The day before I left for Toledo, Dave's wife, Sally, gave a party in my honor with some fifty friends and neighbors in attendance.

During the flight to Toledo my thoughts were mostly about Zan and it seemed as though the flight lasted forever. When we finally landed and I stood in the plane's door, I saw her and her father on the tarmac, smiling and waiting for me. She was wearing a white blouse and a plaid skirt and she looked simply wonderful. Her eyes had that same luminous look that I had noticed five years earlier when I first met her at the cottage on Lake Erie. We hugged and held each other real close without saying anything.

I stayed in Toledo for a week. She and I talked a lot, took walks, played with her cocker-spaniel Tio, and stayed physically close. One day we went horseback riding. Both horses were frisky. The trotting turned into a full gallop. Zan was ahead of me and I saw her going down an incline and then up on a knoll and when I reached that point she was on the ground and the horse was in the distance still galloping. Mine was in full gallop also and seconds later I fell off. The horse kept going. I wasn't hurt, but the fall did something to her lower back that bothered her for many years.

That evening, like the ones before, we cuddled on the living room sofa. I was not very good at making small talk. I remember saying something like "Well, what about it? We're gonna get married, aren't we?" She just nodded, smiling, her eyes as luminous as always. It was a pretty crude proposal, but by then I had become somewhat cocky. The word "insufferable" probably describes it better. We agreed to get engaged but we'd be sensible. We'd wait until the war was over, I was out of the navy, and she had graduated from Oberlin before getting married.

I finally arrived home in Arlington, New Jersey and of course Mother and Dad couldn't do enough for me. Most of my old friends from high school were in the service somewhere. Steve was back in the Pacific on the jeep aircraft carrier *Shipley Bay*. The war was still raging and I kept thinking about the 648, wondering where she was and what she was doing. I felt restless, at loose ends, I was constantly thinking of Zan. Mother, an accomplished pianist, played a couple of selections for me that, she said, she'd been practicing for my return. She was hurt because I didn't express more appreciation.

Today, a popular image of World War II is that of young men donning uniforms and risking their lives for freedom. The image is only half correct. Overlooked are the sacrifices that were endured on the home front by ordinary citizens like my mother and dad. The war was a national, unified effort in which everyone—men and women, adults, and children, civilians all—participated. Seniors grew Victory gardens and volunteered as air raid wardens. Some men not drafted because of a physical disability volunteered as auxiliary firefighters and policemen. Children collected rubber, tin cans, and scrap metal. Ladies' auxiliaries made bandages and layettes. They knitted watch caps, socks, and sweaters for the men in uniform. Six million women worked in defense plants and shipyards, popularizing the image of Rosie the Riveter. Tens of thousands of mothers placed gold stars in their windows to honor sons killed in battle. Shoes, sugar, coffee, meat, typewriters, fuel oil, and gasoline were rationed. A "Class A" sticker got you four gallons of gasoline per week. People rode bikes to conserve gasoline. It was impossible to buy a new car. Tires were rationed. Collection barrels with signs "Keys to Victory" were set up in stores for old keys and metal files. Medical care was limited because there was a shortage of doctors. Newspapers endured paper shortages by printing smaller headlines, limiting the size and number of classified ads, and establishing waiting lists for new subscribers. Some butcher shops sold horsemeat. Silk and rayon disappeared and women drew a line down the back of each leg to make it look as though they were wearing silk stockings. You couldn't get tennis shoes because they had rubber soles. The most popular Christmas gift was a War Bond.

Those were the conditions when I returned from the Pacific. Despite the inconveniences and sacrifices, the spirit and morale of all Americans was higher than it had ever been—and since. The feeling of unity was never greater. The United States was winning the war and everyone knew it couldn't last much longer.

My thirty day leave ended and on March 24th I reported to Commander Frederick W. Lemly at SCTC, Miami. He had returned from the Pacific fairly recently himself and we had some things in common. He had been commanding officer of the APD 16, USS *Ward* which had operated with us in the Aitape and Cape Gloucester landings. The interview with Cmdr Lemly was satisfactory and he told me to to wait for orders that would be forthcoming in a day or two. He indicated I would probably be attached to SCTC as an instructor or in an administrative capacity. Unbeknown to both of us, Cmdr. Lemly would later perform a very big favor for me.

Jerry Lively was also back in the states, attached to SCTC in an administrative job. Paul Spaugh, newly married, was also there. Of course I wasted no time looking up both of them. Jerry still didn't want anything to do with Paul. Many of the officers attached to SCTC had served overseas and lived in apartments in Miami Beach. Everyone realized the duty was temporary and that we'd be reassigned to another ship in three to six months as commanding officers or execs on DEs or DDs. Even though we were winning the war both in Europe and in the Pacific, we couldn't be sure of anything. Many of us assumed an invasion of the Japanese mainland was going to be necessary to complete the war in Japan.

Jerry and his wife Selma lived in a small apartment house called the Drexel Arms on Fourteenth Street, Miami Beach. An efficiency apartment in the Drexel Arms was available, so I rented it. It had a Murphy bed that folded into one wall, a built-in refrigerator and stove on another wall, a chair, a sofa, and a few other meager appointments, but it would suffice.

After three days of settling down, I received a call from Cmdr. Lemly telling me to come see him. When I entered his office he said, "Treadwell, this just came in." and handed me a paper, frowning.

It was a letter to me from COMSERFORSOWESTPAC (Commander, Service Force Southwest Pacific). that had been forwarded to SCTC:

> 6 February, 1945
> Subject: Official Letter of Reprimand
> To: Lieut. Theodore R. Treadwell D(V)G
>
> 1. On 12 January, 1945, Captain Francis W. Caffrey, Commanding Officer of the S.S.Thomas P. Leathers reported that you attempted to appropriate a motor

lifeboat belonging to his ship. You falsely claimed it as belonging to your ship. When he submitted proof of ownership you denied it.

2. Captain Caffrey further reported that when he did recover the boat from you there were several pieces of gear missing, including the boat's compass and an axe.

3. After careful review of this matter it has been determined that your conduct amounted to an attempt to steal property that did not belong to you. Accordingly, your conduct was unbecoming and unwarranted for an officer of the United States Navy.

4. Consider this as an Official Letter of Reprimand, which, together with your acknowledgement and reply, will be made a part of your permanent Qualifications Jacket and Fitness Report file.

Robert O. Glover, RADM USN,
Commander Seventh Fleet Service Force."

I looked at Lemly, shaking my head, hardly believing what I had just read. That merchant captain meant what he said when he yelled "You haven't heard the last of this!"

"What's this all about?" Lemly asked.

I told him the whole story, including the fact I wasn't proud of it, but that I was thinking of my men's morale at the time. I told him how we had to beg, borrow, and moonlight in order to keep going. As I talked he nodded in sympathy and agreement. Fortunately, he had been out there himself and knew the conditions firsthand.

"OK," he said, "It's too bad, but as far as I'm concerned it doesn't affect your immediate future here. Your problem right now is that this letter will become a permanent part of your navy record and the next time you're up for promotion you could be passed over. Down the line if you make the navy your career it could hurt you. You have the right to answer these charges in writing and place it in your file along with the letter, so that if and when you're being considered for a promotion or new assignment, whatever you say in your response will be given equal consideration. So my suggestion is to write an answer to the admiral's charge and bring it in to me. In the meantime, we'll assign you as an afloat instructor in gunnery and seamanship. You can get the details from the Training Office, OK?"

I was lucky that the commander had been out there and knew how things were with most of the subchasers, but the letter was disturbing. Though I didn't plan to make the navy my career, it was a blot that no one wants on his record. To this day I believe the admiral was rather impulsive, since he had heard only one side of the story. Not that I wasn't ashamed or didn't regret my action, however.

I returned to the apartment and composed a lengthy statement in my defense. I wrote about the difficulties faced by SCs when it came to getting supplies, food, and spare parts. I wrote about two SC skippers who committed suicide, another attempting suicide, and a fourth case, a "Section 8," in which the skipper had to be restrained and taken to a mental hospital.

My letter was outlandish and totally unsuitable, and I knew it. I was venting, writing about unrelated things that I felt deeply. I brought it in and handed it to Commander Lemly anyway.

He didn't even finish reading it before looking up, exclaiming, "Treadwell, you can't say these things! They'll crucify you!"

"Yeah, but those things are true, commander."

"It doesn't matter. I'm not going to let you do this."

He finished reading it, shaking his head.

"Tell you what," he finally said, "Leave this with me. I'll try writing an appropriate reply myself. Is that OK?"

"Well, sure, commander, it's fine with me, and thanks. I just want to shake it off and get on with things."

We left it at that and a day or two later I became a member of the faculty of SCTC.

As an afloat instructor I went aboard a destroyer or a destroyer escort—both attached to SCTC as training ships—for five days at sea, instructing groups of new ensigns (most of them as starry eyed as I had been almost three years previously) in gunnery and seamanship. The cruise was their "graduation" exercise, taken after they had completed their classroom training and before being assigned to ships.

At the end of the first cruise I returned to my apartment for the weekend. The weather was beautiful, with bright sunshine, birds singing, bees buzzing, and flowers blooming. Most of the apartments in the Drexel Arms were occupied by married officers, many of them very newly married. It seemed as though I was the only bachelor in the entire Drexel Arms. I began thinking how wonderful it would be for Zan to be with me. I began to rationalize. I began thinking our pledge to wait until the war was over and she had finished college wasn't so sensible after all. She could always finish college later. Nobody knew how long the war would last.

In those days no one even dreamed of an unmarried "relationship." You either married or you stayed single. I rationalized myself into deciding we should get married immediately. I sent her a telegram. It read: "I love you. Will you marry me now, in Miami? Please call and let me know."

There was no telephone in my room but there was a pay phone in the little lobby of the Drexel Arms. I knew things were going to pop at the house in Toledo when they got the telegram so I fetched a chair from my room and sat next to the pay phone waiting for it to ring. It rang about an hour later. Her mother and father were on one phone, Zan on another. The first thing I asked her was whether she wanted to marry me right away. When she said "Yes," I knew it would happen.

Her mother and father were pretty good about it, considering the suddenness of this development.. They said things like "What happened to your promise to wait until the war's over?" and "Do you know what you're doing?" and "Are you both sure?" Her mother said emphatically, "You know, she's still a young girl!" and I replied that she seemed pretty mature to me.

Newlyweds

The conversation finally turned positive and they agreed to it. They would come down and I'd call my parents and have them come. It would be a proper church wedding. I was to set the date and begin making arrangements.

I was the luckiest guy in the world, and the world was coming up roses!

I'll never forget her as she stepped down from the Pullman car, smiling at me and looking so beautiful! We were married on April 7, 1945, in the Miami Beach Community Church. My dad and mother came, Jerry was my best man, and Selma Lively was Zan's matron of honor. Zan's father took us to a nice restaurant for a celebration dinner and in the rented car Zan sat on my lap and we smooched up a storm.

Selma and Jerry Lively April 7, 1945

Our life in that little one-room efficiency apartment was idyllic except for my Monday to Friday sea duty, which meant we were only able to spend weekends together, but we made the most of it. We sailed, socialized with other navy couples, had the Livelys for dinner, entertained the Spaughs at dinner. The beach was only two blocks away. We shopped in little grocery stores and Zan taught me how to cook. We took long walks along stylish Lincoln Boulevard.

A few weeks after we were married, Germany surrendered, and the war in Europe was over.The allies turned their full attention to the war in the Pacific, and it was obvious that Japan was losing.

Early one evening we were strolling on Lincoln Boulevard. We passed a newsboy hawking the Miami Herald, holding up copies and yelling, "Extra! Extra! Read all about it! Atom bomb dropped on Japan!" We bought the paper and in the story was a reference to the Hanford Works near Richland in the state of Washington. It was there where the reactor for the bomb had been developed. This was why my brother Dave couldn't—and wouldn't—talk about what he was doing when I visited him in February. Development of the bomb had been named the Manhattan Project and Dave was intensely involved in it. A week later a second bomb was dropped on Nagasaki. On August 15 Japan surrendered and the Pacific war was suddenly over. People celebrated in the streets, bars, hotels, everywhere. World War II was finally over!

Subchaser Training Center, (SCTC) Miami
National Archives (80G-40338)

The end of my navy career was now in sight, although it took a while for things to wind down from a wartime economy to peacetime. I continued with SCTC for a couple of months as an afloat instructor, and Zan and I made the most of our waning time in Miami Beach. My orders for separation didn't arrive until late in November.

On the day before leaving Miami to go to Jacksonville for official separation from the navy, I stopped at my mailbox at SCTC to pick up the last of any remaining mail. In the box was a thick sheaf of papers with a note attached, which read: "Thought you might want this. Good luck to you as you return to civilian life. Fred Lemly."

The commander had kept all my papers exactly as we had left them in his office and was now returning them to me. The Official Letter of Reprimand from Admiral Glover was there, as was my entire service file.

Because of Commander Lemly's kindness, the Letter of Reprimand never became an official part of my service record. As this began to sink in a wave of gratitude swept over me. Cmdr Lemle had done me an immense favor and I've always been grateful.

Zan and I proceeded to Jacksonville, FL, where, on December 4, 1945, I was officially separated from the navy and placed on inactive duty in the naval reserve.

Last Days of SC 648

When John W. Storrs relieved me of command at Manus on February 3, 1945 the 648 had already been docked for over a month. The ship remained in Manus two more months after that, waiting for engine liners, new sonar gear, and radar. Her total time in port extended to three and one-half months—an unusually long period of inactivity for a subchaser in the Pacific.

April 12—SC 648 departed Manus and sailed to Hollandia, still without radar.

April 19—SC 648 escorted a convoy of tugboats to Leyte. Each tug had a barge in tow, reducing the convoy's speed to 5 knots. The voyage took eleven days.

From March 3 to March 14, new radar that arrived just before leaving Manus was installed.

May 14—Sonar gear tested, found to be not in operating condition."

May 24—Ensign Robert H. Rawlings reported aboard to replace Glenn F. Welsh as third officer.

In late June, SC 648 escorted three small Australian cargo ships to re-supply a recent Australian Army amphibious operation on the coast of Borneo. Mr. Rawlings recalls those ships as being so tiny and obsolete they reminded him of the Nina, the Pinta, and the Santa Maria.

After a brief stay at the island of Tawi Tawi the convoy continued. It was during this voyage that the 648 spotted a floating mine and just barely managed to warn the other ships of its presence. The mine was dispatched by blowing it up with gunfire. The convoy also encountered a typhoon that, according to Rawlings, "tossed the ships about like corks in a washing machine"

On July 4, 1945 the convoy arrived at Victoria Harbor, Brunei Bay, Borneo.

For the next month and a half SC 648 performed escort and patrol duties in the vicinity of Brunei Bay. By now most of the men with whom I had sailed were no longer aboard, having been detached and replaced by youngsters fresh from the states.

On August 6, 1945 the United States dropped the atomic bomb on Hiroshima, and on August 9 another at Nagasaki.

On August 15, 1945, Japan surrendered and the war was over.

In an article Ensign Rawlings wrote in 2000 describing his navy experiences, he reveals how the crew of the 648 received the surrender news and what happened afterwards:

> The ship had patrolled the Pacific off Borneo until the Japanese surrender on August 15. On that particular day, the little ship was anchored in the Bay of Brunei. The men all hovered about the radio when the news came and there were some whoops and shaking of hands but there was no raucous celebration aboard, no champagne poured over the skipper's head. There was, in fact, not even a warm beer to share. The sailors were happy, of course, that the war was over and they had survived, but instead of rejoicing loudly, most quietly wrote letters, thinking of home and families and wondering what the future would hold for them, now that they could again be pretty sure they had a future.
>
> On September 3 documents were signed aboard the battleship Missouri, in Tokyo Bay. The 648 was ordered to convoy with an Australian corvette, several PCs, SCs and PT boats, to proceed up the Sarawak River to rescue a large contingent of British, Dutch and Australian prisoners of war and other Caucasians who had been

interred by the Japanese in jungle concentration camps for nearly five years. Other ships were too big to navigate the narrow and shallow waterway so they waited, together with a large hospital ship, in Sarawak Bay.

September 14, 1945—A rare photo of SC 648 loaded with British and Australian prisoners of war, leaving the wharf at Kuching for the hospital ship Wanganella, stationed at the mouth of the Sarawak River. Photo courtesy of Australian War Memorial, Negative No. 118696

The convoy remained for several days in Kuching. We worked with the POWs and in the process learned how terrible the conditions in the camp had been for the people incarcerated. Not only had they been forced to live in the most miserable of circumstances but the Japanese had beaten them at the slightest excuse. Even though the Japs had started to feed the prisoners reasonably well in the past few weeks, knowing that they would have to turn them over to the US soon, the men were still emaciated and sick. Because they were all wearing shorts and in most cases an unbuttoned shirt, I could see the effects of starvation. Their thighs were simply skin and bone, but their calves and feet were swollen and puffy to almost twice their normal size. It was a heart-rending experience.

We three officers [Storrs, Speier and Rawlings] wandered through the old Chinese city where we were greeted by the Chinese merchants as saviors. One shopkeeper invited us for tea upstairs where his family resided above his store. While we were drinking and chatting I heard some slight giggles coming from the end of the room and looked over to see two very cute Chinese girls who turned out to be the shopkeeper's daughters. He offered his daughters to us and it appeared that they were eager, but all three of us kindly dissented. We knew that these same girls had been offered to and no doubt accepted by Japanese officers.

In all my life that [POW rescue] is my single most unforgettable experience. It made me weep then and, yes, I weep now as I recall that emotional experience.

Rawlings says the experience made him even more aware of the importance of freedom and of the sacrifices sometimes required to protect it. He states that some of his decisions later in life while espousing unpopular or risky causes were undoubtedly influenced by the POW experience.

On October 1, 1945 an army officer with nine enlisted men boarded SC 648 as passengers to Subic Bay. The 648 arrived there on October 5. Several men were transferred off, including three who had served under me. (Atherton, Stewart, and Woodside.) On October 12 the ship once again was laid up for repair and engine overhaul.

On October 17 Ensign Phillip H. Kelber reported aboard for duty as Third Officer.

On October 25 Lt(jg) Woodrow W. Speier was detached, having served his entire sixteen months aboard as executive officer.

On October 26 the ship came out of drydock and made a trial run in Subic Bay. She remained moored or anchored during all of November.

On December 5, 1945 John W. Storrs was relieved of command by Lt(jg) Phillip Kelber.

On December 14 the ship sailed to Manila Bay, P.I.

On December 21 the ship returned to Subic Bay.

On December 22 the ship's ammunition was jettisoned in 175 fathoms of water approximately eleven miles offshore. The next few days were spent transferring men off the ship to barracks at the base in Subic Bay.

On January 26 1946 the crews quarters were secured.

On January 29 SC 648 was towed to dry dock to remove sound gear and fathometer.

On February 5 an inspection party boarded and, in accordance with instructions issued by Commandant U.S. Naval Operating Base, Subic Bay, the SC 648 was decommissioned.

On June 30, 1948 the U.S.S. SC 648 was transferred to China.

(Note: Numerous attempts to communicate with officials in China regarding the ultimate fate of SC 648 have been unsuccessful.)

Last Days of SC 648 209

SC 648 Ship's Company September 1945 (ca)

(Left to right)
Front row kneeling: Page, G.Green, Stewart, VanKirk

Second row: Beebe, Beanblossom, Furman, Atherton, Belcher, Keltner, Shaughnessy, J.Green, L.George, Carnago

Third row: Lt.(jg) W.W.Speir, Exec.Officer, Ens.G.F.Welsh, Third Officer (white t-shirt), Esser, McFall, Woodside, Gallant, Kennedy

Top Row: Dreyer, London, Beck, Eberhardt

APPENDIX A

Capsules

Following, in alphabetical order, are brief bios about a few of the people who crossed my path in this book. Unfortunately, too many are either lost or departed, therefore are not included.

BANE, M. RAY.—"Bane" is still alive and well, living in Bay St. Louis, Mississippi. As a youngster on the 648 he was continually in one scrape or another and when he finally left the ship none of the officers figured he would amount to much—but how mistaken we were! In a letter dated October 18, 2006, he writes: "After the navy I came back to Fort Worth, Texas, went to work for the weather bureau, married, had three children. Attended and graduated (1949) on the G.I. Bill with a B.A. in geology from Texas Christian University in Fort Worth. On a visit to my wife's family in Pasadena, California, I accepted a job working in a core lab, handling cores from Venezuela. I took graduate courses in micropaleontology at USC in Los Angeles. Union of California hired me as a micro-paleontologist; I relocated to Houston, Texas and worked for them about three years. I then went to work for Placid, or Hunt Oil Co. After a few years I left Placid and set up a consulting firm in New Orleans and Lafayette, Louisiana. At age 70 I sold my business, keeping some of the interest, and retired! My wife passed away in 1995. I married Glenda in 2000. I had gone to graduate school with Will (her husband) and had been in their wedding in 1955. Our families knew each other very well and had stayed in touch over these years. The 'Good Man' upstairs has given me many blessings!"

BEANBLOSSOM, ETHBERT.—"Beanie" was our pharmacist's mate, a popular member of ship's company. In a phone conversation with him in September 1994 he told me he never stayed in the hospital business but instead worked for Boise-Cascade in Oregon doing "hunky" work. He was married to Marilyn, and on retirement settled down in Victorville, California. Their son Bob is an airline pilot. Beanie died in March, 1995.

BEEBE, RALPH C. JR.—Ralph completed his education at Ohio Northern and became an electrical engineer. He made a career with Goodyear Aerospace, first in Akron, Ohio, then in New Mexico, finally relocating to Phoenix in 1956. He was married to Alice and they had two daughters. He retired in 1988. Ralph died in April, 1997, after a lengthy illness.

COX, ARNETT GALE.—After the war, Gale Cox settled down in St. Clairsville, Ohio, and worked in West Virginia coal mines for 34 years underground and 10 more years as a foreman, above ground. He served for 23 months aboard SC 648. As a gunner's mate on the 648 his station at General Quarters was first loader on the 40mm gun. During an encounter with enemy planes in Leyte Gulf, another subchaser alongside the 648 fired its 3inch-50 cannon directly over the 648's gun crew, knocking them to the deck. In 1994 Cox wrote to me about this: "All I remember was a red flash and coming to on the deck. Blood was coming out both of my ears and I was laid up for a week on a hospital ship." Later in the same letter: "I will never forget the 648, it was like home. We had a lot of bad times and a lot of good times and a hell of a lot of scary times.

We had a good crew and I was proud to serve with them, through the good and the bad. You were a very understanding skipper, the crew and the officers got along, I don't remember anyone having an argument, and the trust among everyone was super." Arnett Gale Cox died May 11, 2005, at the age of 79.

EBERHARDT, FRED E.—After leaving the navy Fred attended the University of Wisconsin and Chicago Technical College. His working years were spent in commercial construction and as a building estimator in his home city of Manitowoc, Wisconsin. Still in good health, he's been retired for 21 years and enjoys golfing, bowling, and playing cards. He has been married to Beatrice for 58 years and they have three children and one granddaughter. Fred was aboard when the 648 was in Kuching, Borneo, and actively participated in the release of the POWs.

FAGAN, ROBERT F.—As one of the plank owners of SC 648 Fagan was an outstanding ship's cook. His ability to convert dehydrated wartime fare into edible—and many times flavorful—dishes was extraordinary. After the war he exploited his talent by opening a restaurant in his home state of Delaware. When he retired 42 years later he owned eight popular restaurants. He was well known by everyone in the food business and for several years served as the first president of the Delaware Restaurant Owners Association. He married twice and divorced twice. He had eight children. By the time I caught up with him in 1996, he had retired from the restaurant business and returned to his love of reading by opening a small bookstore in Wilmington. Bob Fagan died circa 1998–99.

FIRESTINE, DELBERT E.—"Sparky" was the 648's electrician until receiving a medical discharge in May 1944. He was a railway signal engineer in New York City for 23 years, retiring in 1966. He and his wife Mary moved to Raymond, Ohio. He died in November 1994 after a long illness.

FURMAN, EDWARD R.—Ed is retired and still in good health and spirits. He lives in Cleveland, where he was associated for many years with a large accounting firm. He and his wife have been married for 60 years. They have four sons and five grandchildren. Ed and his wife have always been active in 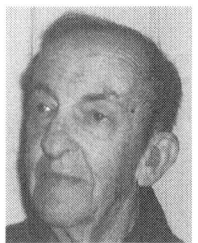 church work and as a hobby he has built many different kinds of birdhouses.

GEORGE, LOUIS.—Lou married Laura, settled in Struthers, Ohio, and worked for many years for Sharon Steel Company as an overhead crane operator. He had four children, several grandchildren, and two great-grandchildren. He retired in 1981 and became an enthusiastic gardener. In the few short years that he and I renewed acquaintance he wrote several long, warm, articulate letters. Lou died in September 2000.

GREEN, GEORGE H.—George Green worked for many years in construction, and died in Albany, New York in 1990.

 GREEN, JAY Q.—Jay has lived in upstate Greenwich, New York, all his life. After the war he and his twin brother Jack boxed professionally. Jay fought 36 fights, losing only one. He worked several years with the New York State Department of Entomology, assisting with ecological problems such as gypsy moths and pine rust. He then became an operating engineer in the construction industry. Thirty-five years

later he retired to enjoy and exploit his hobbies of chess and dendrology. He taught fifth and sixth graders how to play chess and for several years he guided nature "rambles" with teachers and students, exploring the mysteries of native trees and shrubs. I had the great and memorable pleasure of visiting Jay and his wife Valerie in 1995 and both of them are still going strong today.

HODGES, STEPHEN B.—Steve earned his wings in the Navy in August, 1942. He was sent to the South Pacific, where he lived five months on Guadalcanal in tents and foxholes while flying scoutimg missions from Henderson Field. Once he flew General Lawton Collins at low altitude over Japanese lines. (Collins, after the war, became Chief of Staff in Washington, D.C.) He contracted malaria at Guadalcanal and was sent back to the states for recovery, which took until January 1944. He was then assigned to CVE-85, *Shipley Bay*, as Flight Deck Officer and Assistant Air Officer. The *Shipley Bay* supported ground troops during the landing at Okinawa. Steve was promoted to Lieutenant and received a special commendation letter from Captain Austin Wheelock for flight control operations. On July 5, 1946 Steve married Zan's sister Marjorie Ward, thereby elevating our lifelong friendship to brothers-in-law. In 1949 they moved to Bradford, Pennsylvania and have lived there ever since. He worked first for Dresser Industries and then became a branch manager for First Albany, Inc., a brokerage firm, from which he retired in 1988. The Hodges have five children and fifteen grandchildren. Their lifelong church, community, and volunteer activities in Bradford are legion.

HULSE, JOHN K. JR.—Tall, scholarly (he left Lafayette College in his third year to join the navy), soft-spoken and dependable, John earned the respect of everyone as the 648's quartermaster. After leaving the 648 he was assigned to CVE 80, *Petrof Bay*, participating in the Leyte invasion and surviving several close calls with torpedoes and Kamikazes in the Battle of Samar. At Okinawa she withstood the constant onslaught of Kamikazes for 72 days and nights without a scratch, though there were many close calls. On *Petrof Bay* John Hulse was in charge of 16 men, the leading petty officer on the bridge. After the war Hulse earned a B.A. at Lafayette and L.L.B. at Rutgers. He practiced law for more than 40 years in Moorestown, New Jersey. John died circa 1997-.

KENNEDY, ALEXANDER, JR.—Alex set some kind of record by serving aboard SC 648 for more than three years! He was a very able, dependable member of the "Black Gang." Alex also served for three years in the Korean War. He settled in Philadelphia and worked for Atlantic Refining Co. for many years before retiring in 1977. He was active in The Improved Order of Red Men, a patriotic fraternity chartered by Congress. Alex was married for 68 years. They had one son, Donald, five grandchildren, and nine great-grandchildren. Alex died May 1, 2000, at the age of 92.

LIVELY, GERALD M.—"Jerry" and his wife Selma settled down in Prairie Village, Kansas, where he established a lifetime law practice. For many years we kept in touch by Christmas cards. Jerry died in 2004.

RAWLINGS, ROBERT H.—Bob served on the 648 six months, first as Third Officer, then as Executive Officer, during the closing stages of the war. He was an active participant in the mini-surrender and the POW release in Kuching, Borneo. After separation from the navy he returned to Colorado College, graduating in 1947. That same year he began a career with The Pueblo Chieftain, southeastern Colorado's major daily newspaper. In 1980 he became publisher and editor. In

1984 he was elected president of the Star-Journal Publishing Corporation. Bob has had a distinguished career, not only in the publishing business but in many other community affairs. His resume reads like a Who's Who in America, with many honors and citations such as "Outstanding Professional for 1980," "Colorado Newspaper Person of the Year," "Distinguished University Fellow," "1993 Outstanding Citizen of the Year," "1994 Colorado Business Leader of the Year," and many more. He has been married to Mary Alexandra Graham since 1947 and has four children. He is very active as a board member of numerous foundations and corporations and still finds time for an occasional game of golf.

SMITH, ENOCH E.—"Smitty" was one of our radiomen, soft-spoken and a good sailor. After the war he worked for the Bell telephone system in Tennessee. He and his wife Margie had four children and thirteen grandchildren. He died circa 1994.

SPAUGH, PAUL ALLEN—One of the most colorful persons I ever knew, he was born in Dallas, a thoroughgoing Texan. Orphaned at an early age, he had a troubled childhood, but he overcame this and gained admission to Texas A & M University. There, he worked in the laundry for four years while majoring in accounting and finance and excelling as a member of the A-&-M swim team. After graduating in 1939 he worked for Humble Oil Co. and also picked up some small boat experience, the latter standing him in good stead at SCTC, placing him in the "Captains in Training" class while there. After the war he made a career with Standard Oil Company (ESSO, later EXXON), starting as a rigger in the oil fields. He spent most of his working years in Brazil (Rio de Janeiro and Sao Paulo). He died of a heart attack on April 23, 1979 at the age of 60. At the time of his death he was president of ESSO Chemical Company,

South America. We are indebted to his widow, Marilyn Spaugh for this information about Paul.

STENGELE, FRANCIS J.—Certain members of a ship's company are remembered for nothing more than their character and personality. Stengele had both. Born and raised in the Bronx, NY, he never completed high school. After the war, he made a career working for Western Electric Co. and AT&T. His first wife of 42 years died in 1987. In 1995, when he and I caught up with each other at his home in Islamorada, Florida, he had recently married Kathy Graves and was just as enthusiastic about fishing as ever. Frank Stengele died in 2000.

SWETT, CLINTON T.—Swett died of cancer in 1980 in Lake Worth, Florida. He was married and had a daughter. His widow was still living in 1994.

TREADWELL, ELIZABETH W.—"Zan" and I were happily married for 39 years until she was taken by ovarian cancer at the age of 61. We had five children and Zan dedicated her life to them. After Andrew, our son with Down Syndrome, was born in 1958, she devoted a major part of her time as an advocate for de-institutionalization and equal human rights for all. Thanks to her efforts, Andy today possesses high reading skills, lives semi-independently, and is a happy adult. Her love of nature and her curiosity about many different things never ceased to amaze me. I yanked her out of Oberlin to get married, but many years later, after our children had flown the coop, she earned her B.A. degree in English at Framingham State College, Framingham, Massachusetts. Zan was an inspiration to everyone who knew her.

TREADWELL, DAVID R.—My older brother, a chemical engineer, had an illustrious career with E. I. DuPont de Nemours & Company. During the war he was in Richland,

WA, a key player in the Manhattan Project. Later, he was the manager of DuPont's first Teflon plant, and for many years was known as "Mr. Teflon." He and his wife, Sally, had three children. Dave retired in 1977 and settled in Wilmington, Delaware, where today, at the ripe old age of 95, he wins more often than he loses at blackjack in nearby Atlantic City. His lifelong hobby has been contract bridge, having been awarded the title of Grand Life Master and election to the Hall of Fame of the American Contract Bridge League. He recently achieved a lifetime goal of more than 25,000 masterpoints, placing him 25th on the all-time list of masterpoint holders. His penchant for telling corny jokes, a character defect borne bravely by family members, is almost as well known as his reputation as a world-class bridge player,

VERNOR, RICHARD E.—Dick and I met each other fifty-four years after our job-swap in Noumea, at a PCSA (Patrol Craft Sailors Association) reunion in Virginia Beach. Dick served 27 months in the Pacific. He inspected Armed Guard units in Noumea for a while, then was transferred to Guam as Gunnery Officer. He finally was assigned to the aircraft carrier *Shangri-La*, where he was OOD Watch Stander in Port and Underway, as well as Sector Control Officer on the 20 and 40mm guns. A lawyer by profession, Dick was admitted to the U.S. Supreme Court Bar. For many years he was assistant general counsel of the Washington office of the American Life Convention. Dick and his wife raised three daughters and, since his wife's death in 1974, he has helped raise five grandchildren. He has engaged in volunteer work in the community for more years than he can remember and still plays a round of what he modestly says is "poor" golf.

WAWROSKI, STAN—Thanks to the Internet Stan and I caught up with each other very recently. Most of the time during the war "Doc" Wawroski was stationed in Darwin, Australia as a bomb disposal officer. He participated in several mine laying operations throughout the southwest Pacific and in the Philippines. In June, 1944 he married Martie Paton, an Australian, in Brisbane. After the war Stan obtained his dentistry degree from Loyola University. In 1951 he moved to the Monterey Bay area, where he practiced Oral/Maxillofacial surgery for the remainder of his career. Stan served on the Monterey Peninsula College Board of Trustees and was active in several community service organizations. In his younger days he was a talented musician (clarinet) and track athlete. His daughter Beverly has followed Stan's example as a marathon runner. Martie, his wife of 54 years, passed away in 1998. Stan died March 26, 2007.

APPENDIX B
Ship's Roster

Following is a list of everyone who served, no matter how briefly, on SC 648 during her 3-year 7-month life as a U.S. Navy commissioned warship:

[* Plank Owner]
[** Temporary duty]
[NR—not recorded]

Name	*Rate/Rank*	*Dates of service*
Atherton, Fred G.	S2C	11/28/43–10/11/45
Bane, M. Ray	GM3C	02/04/43–08/01/43
Beanblossom, Ethbert	PhM2C	05/21/43–11/01/44
*Beck, Victor F.	Y3C	07/14/42–10/12/44
Beebe, Ralph C. Jr.	QM2C	01/24/43–03/31/45
Belcher, Charles Hayden	SM3C	04/12/44–11/2/44
Braden, Everett W.	S2C	10/16/45–01/22/46
Broussard	SC1/C	01/08/45–01/22/45
Butts, H. S.	S1C	12/13/45–12/28/45
Carnago, Louis J.	S1/C	01/10/44–10/2/45
Coto, Anthony	SoM3C	12/13/45–12/28/45
Cox, Arnett G.	GM2C	12/07/43–11/01/45
Davis, Charles E. Jr.	MM2C	03/13/43–07/17/43
Deking, F.	GM3/C	06/21/44–07/01/44

Name	*Rate/Rank*	*Dates of service*
**Detellem, Donald L.	S1/C(RM)	04/12/44–05/08/44
*Dickenson, Denman A.	CMM(AA)	07/11/42–08/31/42
Distavla, John J.	SC1C	02/13/45–10/11/45
Doyle, Erwin W.	SC3C	01/11/46–01/26/46
Dreyer, Ronald J.	S1/C	08/08/43–10/10/44
Dunn, Willard J.	F2/C	05/23/44–06/22/44
Eastlick, R. E.	S2C	12/13/45–01/26/46
Eberhardt, Fred	RM2C	09/13/44–12/28/45
Effner, John C.	Cox	08/01/43–11/04/43
Esser, Thomas W.	RM1C	09/20/42–04/10/45
Eubank, Hubbard T.	S1C	11/28/43–12/08/43
*Fagan, Robert F.	SC3C	07/11/42–06/24/44
*Fairlie, James T.	MM2C	07/11/42–08/07/44
Firestine, Delbert E.	EM2C	01/20/43–11/03/43
Folster, Kenneth	S1C (QM)	10/17/45–01/26/46
Fredricks, B. E.	RdM3C	01/22/45–12/28/45
Furman, Edward R.	S2C(SM)	08/15/44–03/31/46
Gallant, Leo H.	S/1C(EM)	09/28/44–01/12/45
George, Louis	GM2C	12/04/42–04/10/45
**Gibeson, E. L.	S1/C(RM)	04/12/44–05/02/44
Gilpatrick, H. J.	SC2C	02/05/45–03/31/45
Green, George Henry	S2C	11/15/42–02/09/45
Green, Jay Q.	GM2C	11/15/42–04/10/45
Griggs, Benjamin F.	StM2C	01/11/46–01/26/46
Hachler, C. L.	PhM1C	05/06/45–01/26/45
*Hagmann, Allen E.	MM2C	07/11/42–11/22/43
Harrell, Luther E.	Y2C	10/17/45–01/26/46

Name	Rate/Rank	Dates of service
Headings, D. L.	F2C (EM)	11/21/45–01/17/46
Herrington, William T.	MoMM1C	NR–10/01/45
Hills, Dean D.	F3C	08/01/43–02/29/44
Hintzman, A. M.	RM2C	08/29/42–NR
Horvath, A. J.	F1C	01/08/45–01/05/46
*Hulse, John K.	QM2C	07/11/42–11/03/43
Humphreys, D. X.	GM3C	12/13/45–01/26/46
Irvine, G. E.	F1C	01/22/45–11/01/45
Jaekel, Robert F.	CBM	06/02/45–08/30/45
James, Herby Jr.	BM2	05/23/44–11/29/45
**Jamison, John W.	Capt.(USN)	04/14/44–05/02/44
Jasso, Anthony S.	MM2C	01/20/43–08/01/43
*Joy, Richard P. Jr.	LT(jg) C.O.	07/11/42–12/07/42
Kasarsky, C. P.	S1C	12/13/45–01/26/46
Kelber, Phillip H.	Lt(jg) C.O.	10/17/45–01/26/46
Keltner, Cletus O.	MoMM2C	12/07/43–04/12/45
*Kennedy, Alexander Jr.	F3C	07/04/42–30/08/45
Kovalyesik, N. Jr.	S1C	12/13/45–01/26/46
Landers, Glenn F.	F2C	01/03/45–01/26/46
Lescohier, Donald H.	LT(jg) C.O.	8/16/42–01/23/43
Lively, Gerald M,	Lt. (jg) X.O.	01/20/43–04/17/44
*Lockhart, George H.	MATT3C	07/16/42–12/26/42
London, Robert J.	Cox	09/13/44–12/28/45
*Magaziner, Richard H.	QM3C	07/16/42–01/23/43
Maltsberger, D. L.	SoM3C	04/11/45–12/28/45
Marshall, Richard K.	MoMM1C	10/12/45–01/05/46
*May, Ernest	MM2C	07/11/42–01/18/43

Name	Rate/Rank	Dates of service
McCarthy, Daniel V.	ENS.	12/06/42–01/21/43
McCauley, Russell S.	GM3C	03/12/45–10/11/45
McFall, Gendron	F2C	05/23/44–01/02/45
**McKee, Donald H.	T/3dGR AUS	04/12/44–05/02/44
*Mefford, Paul	GM2C	07/11/42–12/20/43
Merten, Jerome R. Jr.	F1C	12/24/44–02/21/45
Moody, Donald L.	GM3C	12/21/44–01/05/46
Moore, Bobbie	StM2C	10/27/45–11/29/45
Morgan, Raymond J.	GM3C	03/12/45–10/11/45
Mosby, R. H.	S2C	01/18/43–05/29/43
*Moyer, James E.	SoM3C	07/11/42–06/24/44
Natarelli, S.	GM3C	NR–08/30/45
*Newman, Rankin	RM3C	07/11/42–05/14/44
O'dell, Glenn A.	MoMM1C	04/11/45–10/01/45
Page, Guy	F1C	09/19/44–04/10/45
Perkins, G. F.	PhM1C	NR–08/30/45
Pfirter, William E.	EM3C	11/04/43–02/24/44
*Pratt, Arnold A.	CBM	07/11/42–01/23/43
Rambo, Arlen S.	F1C	06/21/44–04/12/45
Rawlings, Robert H.	ENS	05/24/45–12/13/45
*Rice, Heber V.	S/N2C	07/11/42–08/04/44
Rubidoux, F. A.	F1C	01/21//43–03/12/43
*Schmerbeck, Elmer H.	EM1C	07/11/42–02/03/43
Shannon, Walton E.	RdM3C	12/24/44–08/30/45
Shaughnessy, Edward P.Jr.	SC3C	05/23/44–10/10/44
Schroeder, W. F.	RM3C	03/12/45–01/09/46
Smith, Enoch E.	S1C	08/16/44–03/31/45

Name	Rate/Rank	Dates of service
*Smith, Everett W.	MM1C	07/11/42–08/09/43
Smith, J. B.	S1C	10/20/45–01/17/46
Sosbe, Henry W.	S2C	05/11/44–06/22/44
**Soule, R. A.	LT	08/10/42–NR
Spaugh, Paul Allen,	Lt (jg) C.O.	11/15/42–07/14/44
Speir, Woodrow W.	Lt (jg) XO	07/14/44–10/25/45
Stavla, D.	SC1C	02/13/45–01/26/46
*Steiger, Lewis E.	S1C	07/11/42–02/04/43
Stengele, Francis J.	EM2C	12/04/42–08/17/44
*Stephens, Shirley	ENS XO	07/11/42–08/16/42
Stewart, Stanley E.	Cox	06/05/44–10/11/45
John W. Storrs	LT(jg) C.O.	02/03/45–12/05/45
*Swett, Clinton T. Jr.	S2C	07/11/42–02/22/44
*Tackett, John K.	S1C Cox	07/11/42–12/26/42
Tinder, Robert K.	MoMM1C	10/12/45–11/01/45
Touhy, William M.	BM2C	12/25/42–11/06/43
Towns, John	MoMM2C	10/27/45–10/28/45
Treadwell, Theodore R.	LT C.O.	04/24/43–02/03/45
Underwood, W. A.	SoM3C	12/30/44–01/26/46
Unger, Adrain L. Jr.	F1C	03/12/45–10/11/45
Van Kirk, Richard D.	S2C	10/31/43–12/23/44
Vernor, Richard E.	ENS 3d Off.	01/19/43 04/24/43
Vorel, F.	S1C	10/20/45–12/05/45
**Villandry, W. G.	RM2C	08/10/42–08/29/42
Welsh, Glenn F.	ENS 3dOff.	04/12/44–06/04/45
Westring, Charles A.	F3C	07/09/43–04/12/45

Name	Rate/Rank	Dates of service
Wolf, John C.	S1C	11/20/45–01/26/46
Woodside, Earl T.	MoMM2C	05/23/44–10/11/45

About the Author

A native of New Jersey, Theodore "Ted" Treadwell lived most of his life in upstate New York and New England. After graduating from Rutgers University and Harvard Business School, he spent four years in the navy, two of them on a subchaser in the Pacific. After the war he and his wife Zan raised five children while he made a career in the packaging industry, from which he retired in 1984. Not long after that he began researching and writing about the little wooden subchasers.

The years of research sent Treadwell and his sons Dan and Ted III to National Archives, the Naval Historical Center, the Naval Institute, and other facilities throughout the U.S., England, and Norway. Treadwell's Fine Arts model of SC 648 is on display in the Navy Museum in Washington, DC. He continues to write while "fully maturing" at the age of 91, in Bellingham, WA.

The Treadwells maintain a website dedicated to subchasers:

http://www.splinterfleet.org

978-0-595-43860-0
0-595-43860-1

Made in the USA
Lexington, KY
21 January 2017